To
Anne

Remember The F[...]
and H.H. — Then Curtis Brown —
all those memories to share —

Katherine

LONDON ISTANBUL
WITHOUT EVEN A
SCREWDRIVER

Through Tito's Jugoslavia

Katherine Creon

LONDON ISTANBUL WITHOUT EVEN A SCREWDRIVER

Copyright © Katherine Creon 1993

ISBN 1 85863 028 2

First Published 1993 by
MINERVA PRESS
2, Old Brompton Road,
London SW7 3DQ.

Printed in Great Britain

LONDON ISTANBUL

WITHOUT EVEN A SCREWDRIVER

THROUGH TITO'S JUGOSLAVIA

Katherine Creon

DEDICATIONS

Professor Nuriye Pinar-Erdem

and

Madame Turhan Cakus

ACKNOWLEDGMENTS

Jan Siegler and the late John Bourne, for invaluable advice and help.

The Archdeacon of the Aegean and the Danube, the Venerable Geoffrey B. Evans.

Michael Standage - Charles Sturm - Valery Gyöker

Davic Petrovič - Mrs. Leighton James - Eren Ölcüoglu

The Chesham Reference Library

ACCENTS IN SERBO-CROAT

c with an accent is hard = tch.

c with no accent is soft = ts.

For instance the river Pečka-Bistrica is a combination of both, it becomes: Petchska-Bistritsa.

š with an accent becomes = sh as in Niš.

LONDON ISTANBUL
WITHOUT EVEN A SCREWDRIVER

SYNOPSIS

In 1957, on the spur of the moment, having just passed my driving test, I decided to drive to Turkey where I had inherited a large fortune, from a French grandfather, which was held frozen by the authorities.

By the time I found a second hand car and one thing and another we were well into November. I drove through Dalmatia and Montenegro before any roads had yet been made in Jugoslavia, being apparently the very first person to take that route in winter. So the Press said, and over there I was held for a freak and my picture became front page news.

In addition to the unsuspected hazards of the terrain, snow blizzards and such, I also had to contend with modern brigands, eager to do away with the driver to appropriate the car and a few other happenings not scheduled on my route sheet.

However the wild beauty of the country and the art treasures of Jugoslavia, Northern Greece and Turkey were worth any hardship, as were discovering the glory of Byzantium, the magnificence of the Ottoman Empire and a glimpse at the ancient Greek remains of Ephesus being re-excavated for the first time since the beginning of the century.

Subsequently, in the course of many trips by different routes through the same countries up to the 1980s, I was able to observe the customs of each and their cultural, economic and political progress, especially in Turkey, where I went back to stay for ten years.

However at the close of that first visit I had to make a hasty exit with what money I was able to retrieve, before the authorities had time to change their minds when they found out that it was I who had double-crossed them, at their own game in the end!

CONTENTS

Chapter   **Page**

1. Rijeka - Novi   7

2. Gospič- Split   18

3. Dubrovnik   28

4. Kotor - Peč   34

5. Peč - Skopje - Thessaloniki   44

6. Macedonia
   Thessaloniki to the Turkish border   53

7. Edirne - Istanbul   61

8. Aghia Sophia - Pammakaristos   69

9. Byzantium and Constantinople
   Saint Saviour in Chora and other Treasures   77

10. Istanbul and its wonders
    Topkapi Saray   87

11. Turkish Poets   99

12. Ankara - Izmir   108

13. Christmas in Smyrna   116

14. Smyrna named after an Amazon   120

15. Ankara Hosts The Shah of Persia   127

16. How Ever Did Goebbels Get Away With It!   133

LONDON ISTANBUL WITHOUT EVEN A SCREWDRIVER

CHAPTER 1

Rijeka - Novi

"If they lock you up in Jugoslavia get in touch, I'll have you out" that reporter had said in London, as I was starting the car.

"How could I, if I'm locked up?" I had called back.

The year was 1957, the month of November. A few pictures were taken. I could just imagine the caption: 'First woman to drive through Jugoslavia, alone in winter'.

It was later, much later, that I fully appreciated the significance of 'in winter'.

Now, within a few yards of the Jugoslav frontier post, the Iron Curtain! A bunch of unshaven comrades loomed from a haphazard construction, grey and grim. Piercing gazes scanned the contents of the Hillman Husky - the only car within sight and with a woman at the wheel - for signs of the hidden spy amidst the luggage.

Inside the customs house I found myself striving to complete six exact copies of a questionnaire, because I had no visa - which in London was claimed not to be necessary.

"Nije," here a visa was 'de rigueur' plus a substantial fine in dollars for turning up without one.

No sooner had my wheels touched Jugoslav soil than a shrill police whistle made me slam on the brakes. The road was deserted so it could only be for me. Why arrest me now? Why not just refuse me entry?

I ventured a cautious side glance. Yes it was for me. A tall broad man marched purposefully across the road. His long bulky brown overcoat made him look huge. Secret Police! Flat arid country stretched on either side. There was no one about.

He smiled, and pointing to a vast peasant woman following in his wake:

"Per la Mama" he said.

She was dressed in black from the kerchief tied under her chin down to her black stockings and felt slippers.

"Solamente per venti kilometre" he added reassuringly, pointing towards the open road.

Meanwhile la Mama had already let herself into the passenger seat beside me and was arranging her many string bags around her feet. Her son, though he spoke the language of the Italian conquerors of his country, had the blond robust looks of the Austrians who had held Dalmatia on and off throughout the centuries.

La Mama cheerfully waved him good-bye.

"Andiamo."

There was no possible way out. I started the car. She was a jovial, ample woman, who chatted continuously and asked many questions - some of which I grasped. Then turning in her seat, to take a good look at me, she upset her string bags; vegetables and things spilled about the floor and under the seat.

"Sposata?"

"No."

Whereupon she roared her delight, punctuated with a joyous slap on my knee. The car jerked as my foot hit the clutch.

"Never mind," she consoled me, "I have another son *al casa!* You'll see, you'll like him!"

He met us at the door of his café; in the middle of nowhere, off the road to Rijeka. A vine climbed over a concrete terrace where iron chairs were piled on iron tables. This son was the Italianate type, smaller than the other and dark.

"Andiamo" La Mama ordered me out of the car and into the café where I was offered a glass of Slibovitz - plum brandy - in welcome. It left me panting with my throat on fire.

After being shown round the house, we returned to the bar where, over a Jugoslav cigarette, the son gazed at me with eyes of black velvet, and declared me to be:

"Molto sympatica."

La Mama was overjoyed:

"Well?", she roared with a jolly slap on the back that sent me reeling against the bar counter.

To their amazement I began to take my leave.

"But, but, my son, he likes you, *che cosa?"*

I explained, as best I could, that I would return after seeing the rest of Jugoslavia. Perhaps they had waited for me.

Descending into Rijeka along sunny roads bordered with red mounds of earth, rocks and small scattered cottages, I was often stopped by friendly people in lavishly embroidered costume, calling greetings in Italian, insisting I should go and see their village, only up that steep bend, where they'd love me to stay. These spontaneous offers of hospitality followed me all the way. Would the other nineteen million Jugoslavs be so warm hearted?

In Rijeka clanking trams threaded their way through narrow streets, amongst grey concrete buildings. Drab crowds. Drab hotel.

At the Putnik Tourist Office a well intentioned French-speaking young man dashed my hopes of driving to Dubrovnik. No road. Only over mountains. Impossible. The only way was by ferry-boat, going round the islands, but, as it left after three p.m. the next day, I would only see two islands out of one thousand, for it would be dark, and Split at six the following morning, with a stop of ten minutes only! The Shipping agency, he said, was situated along the harbour.

Unsuspected by the casual traveller, the latter day booming Jugoslav Tourist Trade, was already slowly but steadily being engineered. A little way south-west of Rijeka, at the head of the Pula Peninsula, Opatija, to mention only one, was being refurbished for the visitors that up to recently flocked there and marvelled at it's beauty. Its famous Hotel Kvarner, where crowned heads had stayed since the late 1880s, was in the pipe-line to being modernised with care, retaining the charm of its past splendour. In the 1980s, there were three swimming pools, and private bathrooms were easily fitted to its spacious bedrooms. By comparison to the rest of Europe, it was still cheap for what you got! A new road skirted the sea, past the rusty railings of sumptuous villas, whose access to private beaches had been cut off.

Rijeka/Fiume's fortunes had been varied throughout the centuries, a span of a thousand years or so. Fiume means river in Italian and so does Rijeka in Serbo-Croat.

Hungary held the port as firmly as she could, on and off, for it was her only outlet to the sea (as Trieste was to Austria) for her Navy rather than for mercantile purposes. Venice snatched it with Dalmatia to ensure safe passage to her merchant fleet in the Adriatic harassed by

Uskoks, who fleeing from the Turkish onslaught, had taken up piracy to survive.

Fiume was, unbelievably, the scene of a Ruritanian genre play, when the poet D'Annunzio, who owned substantial lands there, seized it in 1919 with a handful of Legionnaires. He managed to hold it for a whole year, after which it remained independent up to 1924. Then it was annexed by Mussolini, and finally handed over to Tito's Jugoslavia by the Allies at the end of the second world war.

A few fishing boats and cutters bobbed gently in the green waters of the harbour presenting splashes of brilliant colours and hard whites under a blazing sun. Nobody about. No shops, no cafés, no loiterers by the water. Only the gritty dry jetty and the cloudless sky, for which I omitted to give thanks, being still very green about driving across Central Europe in November on dirt tracks that can turn to a sea of mud at the first downpour! In an emergency I would not be able to push, for though my spine had improved since I was declared on the point of paralysis five years earlier, I was still wearing a steel orthopaedic corset and carried in the car four firm mattress cushions to lay on the floor of hotel rooms when the bed proved too soft.

On the shady side along the deserted quay there were a few dilapidated buildings, looking abandoned. But there was a shipping agent though the place appeared lifeless, and yes, there was a ferry, if I waited a day or two.

The cost of the trip for AMO 924 and me, was very nearly the price he had cost me second hand. My friends had thought that the number plate alone was worth the price! However when driving through Italy its success could be a trifle overpowering. At one point, followed by cars hooting and voices yelling: 'Signorina perche Amo?' I nearly got out to pull a veil over it!

Behind the next counter, at the shipping office, a dark curly haired little woman watched, bright eyed. She murmured:

"Molto caro."

"Si, molto."

In fact it would swallow up the total amount of dinars I had for my stay of ten days in the country. At that time you were advised to take in cash all the dinars needed on the journey, for when changing travellers cheques locally, the worthless dinar was counted at an exorbitant rate. Perhaps make believe helped them to think they were solvent. After all, such practices might well refill their exchequer if

kept up long enough and tourists flocked in. Most unlikely. So far
there had been no other.

"Why don't you go by road?" the brunette shipping clerk asked
motioning with her chin towards my Hillman standing outside. A car
was a rare thing then in Jugoslavia. I repeated what had been told.

"*Non e vero*, there is a bus that goes all the way, if a bus can do it
so can you."

Then she added with a disdainful look at her male colleagues:

"You don't listen to them, men, ha! They think we can do nothing
on our own!"

"But they say there is no road."

"Who says? There is a road. Not good, but a road. A few bumps
but what's that, the bus gets through, how does it?"

A feminist! But there was something in what she said. And anyway
I could not spare the dinars. Petrol! Where was the petrol station?

Handing over petrol coupons and getting filled up was easy, but
how to ask for the tyres to be checked? A nice young man, a passer by
it seemed, soft hat and long overcoat as the one before, came to my
rescue most obligingly in English.

"To Split? You want to drive to Split?" Eyebrows raised in
disbelief.

"Yes, yes, I know about the state of the road and all that," I
interrupted impatiently, "which way?"

He began to explain, then:

"You will never find it, I will show you."

I cut him short. I had been able to get this far from London, so I
might just manage. Changing his approach, he said dejectedly, he was
an electrical engineer in a factory and had the day off. But what could
he do with a holiday in this place? Nowhere to go, nothing to do. He
would gladly accompany me for a little way and put me on the right
road. No trouble at all, on the contrary, it would be such a change to
have a ride in a car.

"You don't know what it is like to live in a place like this" he
whispered.

"All right" I said.

We left the harbour with its painted small craft, and climbed on to
a kind of corniche road.

"Susak over there. You heard of D'Annunzio, yes? That was his and much more" he made a wide gesture not seeming to share the general distate of Jugoslavs for the poet's excesses in this region.

The water, a few feet below us, was emerald green and so clear that you could see the algae and fish to quite a depth. On our left there were hardly any signs of life, one or two houses, the worse for wear, then just red rock and grass. But the sea view was getting ever more beautiful as we climbed, with a myriad of islands baking in the sun below.

To think that, by the 1980s this coast was full of life with resorts, luxury hotels and a busy thriving population! It took another ten years, well into the 1960s for things to get going.

I suddenly realised that I must drop my passenger soon. He would have a long walk back.

Stopping the car I turned to him. He was busy inspecting the contents of it and fingering everything, particularly my new Rolleiflex camera.

"You must be rich to have all this!"

He went on to tell me with mounting despair, that even though he was a skilled engineer he only got the equivalent of six pence per hour. Could I believe it? He cried.

How was he so well acquainted with the rate of exchange?

He must leave the country, he continued, no future in it.

I immediately thought secret police. Agent provocateur, and remained unresponsive.

He must have a car, a car such as this one. But how? How ever, on six pence an hour! His voice broke. I had an anxious look at him out of the corner of an eye. His features were contorted, he was getting more worked up by the second. Oh dear! I must get rid of him quickly. Leaning over to open the door on his side, I suggested he had better now start on his way back.

He interrupted and waved me on:

"There is a bus."

Flitting across my brain was the thought that he needed to work himself up to get the courage to bash me on the head. There was no one about, not for miles. No fishing boats on the sea. Nothing.

Why was I travelling alone? he asked. Where was I going?

My husband, I invented, was the British Consul in Split. He was expecting me. I was already overdue. Last time this happened he called the police to look for me. No reaction. I had left it too late, he was now too far gone to care. Then he must have known, which I did not, that on this road one could not reach Split. Not for days anyway, over the rugged Karst mountains.

I started the engine, driving slowly, thinking, thinking. We were climbing ever higher on this promontory. Now the water below us could only be seen beyond the tops of the rocks. The view was getting magnificent.

"Stop here!" he screamed, as we rounded up a sharp bend. Sheer cliffs tumbled down to the emerald sea far below. The road opened out wider here. In the 1980s it was turned into a panorama point. Then it was beaten earth, loose at the edges. Most unsafe.

Slamming the door shut, he marched to the very edge of the cliff, bent over forward, gesticulating wildly. He stammered:

"You must see. It is beautiful. Come leave door open."

I put one leg out diffidently, and then it dawned on me! How awful! How stupid of me. Of course!

As he was gesturing towards the chasm below I stepped on the accelerator, leaving the door flapping:

"I'll just get my swim suit on!" I yelled, but realised that in spite of this bravado my blouse was stuck to my back. Fear.

I drove along that narrow ledge of beaten earth turning and twisting and stopped only when well beyond reach to shut the door. Falling back against the seat exhausted, limp, I wiped my face bathed in perspiration. Then kneeling, I frenziedly pulled luggage over from the back of the car and piled it upon the passenger seat. Now everyone could see there was no room for lifts.

The crumbly dirt road meandered on hugging the hill on one side, while to the other commanding a view of red rocks jutting far out to sea. The island of Krk stretched across the Kvarner Bay on a sea where the white fringe of wavelets sparkled in the sun.

What a place to build a house. What heavenly solitude. What scenery. What pure air! But then what else? A life of contemplation, and fish for food. Driving on the Autoput above this road, years later, with all the comforts of the twentieth century within reach, I thought nostalgically back on my first drive as a unique experience.

Eventually I reached Novi, an Adriatic resort, with AMO my faithful companion with whom I occasionally shared my impressions, I shall refer to him henceforth as a friend.

As far as could be seen there was nothing but an hotel prettily nestling against the cliff below, its terrace level with the road, shaded by a trellis vine. It was enchanting.

The van of a film shooting unit barred the way. The driver, a most civilised man, explained in Italian that the road went no further. This was it.

"Dubrovnik?" he looked at me in astonishment, "you can't, well..." he shrugged his shoulders, and finally concluded, "the only way is inland", pointing to a stony, rutted track up the bare mountain which started almost at our feet.

No road? But that woman had said: 'Don't listen to them, buses do it so why can't you', buses do it? Another incredulous look up that track. How could they?

Oh well, I might as well have a coffee. Stepping down to the hotel terrace with one more lingering glance at the forbidding track, I was soon hobnobbing with the stars who climbed up from the rocks, during an interval, to meet this stranger travelling alone in the wilderness.

The women were very pretty with that feline grace not now found in the West. The men tall, and yes, dark and handsome. Some spoke Italian others French. When they left me to resume filming, I noticed the coffee tasted of roasted chick peas.

The driver of the van, convinced he had put me off, lit another cigarette leaning against the bonnet of his vehicle in the sun. It was warm for November. What was it like in England now? Did I feel a tiny bit lonely, all by myself in the middle of nowhere?

It was now well over a week since I had left London. The purpose of this journey was twofold, one was cultural, to see the Byzantine frescoes in Jugoslavia, Greece and Byzantium itself Constantinople - Istanbul, the other purpose a material one, which I tended to lose sight of - to try and persuade the Turks to release my money recently frozen there. My French maternal grandfather had misguidedly invested his fortune in property in Smyrna, in the good old days when it was a beautiful cosmopolitan city - some of which I inherited. My mother's sister who was on the spot at the time, wrote that it was impossible to unfreeze it. A word I found indigestible, and so I decided on the spur of the moment, to drive there to assess the situation.

The Hillman Husky acquired in haste second hand, or rather a few hands removed, from a service man who had bought it in Cyprus, behaved well, even in my inexperienced hands. I had only recently passed my driving test. My instructor's parting words: 'Practice is the best teacher'. Well then after travelling these three thousand miles to my destination I should have learnt.

The preparations for this trip were limited and basic. My provisions consisted of tins of spam, cheese, biscuits, instant coffee, tea, milk powder, sugar, fruit. A kettle to plug on the battery, which proved absolutely marvellous, water could be boiled while driving - on smooth surfaces of course. Three firm Dunlopillo cushions to sleep on when hotel beds did not suit my bad back. Sheets and towel, after I had been warned that in Jugoslavia comrades were expected to share these commodities in hotels. A rug. A map of Europe on which roads, even in Jugoslavia, looked good, and A.A. route sheets of the places I had chosen to visit. However I had been warned never to venture on a road not marked on them, and definitely never upon a bridge which might look good but could cave in under a car's weight. As far as the information available by 1957, the ones indicated on my sheet should just be adequate. One or two travellers in London, who had gone through via Zagreb, Belgrade, the usual route then, warned of hardship in case of mud, advising a ground sheet to spread under the wheels should they become bogged in. Another arranged a meeting at her house in Chelsea, with Lord Kinross, who had travelled throughout Turkey by rickety bus and written those fascinating travel books some of which I had read. He urged me not to miss seeing Ayvalik, a delightful village along an emerald sea, with red rock and pine. I was to see it many times on another visit. That road led eventually to Edirne, through the Dardanelles, but was a military area for which a permit could be obtained. He had done it.

I had read a travel book on Jugoslavia, which fired my imagination, by a couple who wrote of the places they had seen (they had done it in summer) discussing the beauty of the frescoes, but nothing about the way to get there.

Now I was engaged on this venture, I had to admit it was shaping out differently from a ride in the lanes of Buckinghamshire!

Novi was supposed to be an interesting Mediaeval stronghold with a thirteenth century Francopan castle. Where could that castle be? The world seemed to end with this dirt road. No other way. More than ten years had elapsed since the end of the war, and everything seemed to have remained static, both in Rijeka and elsewhere. That feeling of 'after the war' prevailed. Of course, they were free and united for the first time in a thousand years.

Throughout the centuries they contended with one another: Croats, Serbs, Dalmatians, Montenegrins, Slovenes, Bosnians, and with the great powers - Austria, Hungary, the Republic of Venice, who ruled over them in turn. Then they had to fight the Turks in the fifteenth century. The French, under Napoleon, had been their overlords for a brief period of eight years, and then it all started over again until Mussolini's Italy.

They struggled against the Nazis, and Tito's personality brought them together. Since Tito's death, internecine struggle has flared up again. Recently in 1987, this situation had been aggravated in the autonomous province of Kosovo, by Albanians there, who can hardly be described as a minority, as they number well over a million against the two hundred thousand Serbs.

In 1957 however, the people could look ahead to a new life, to build, exploit their natural resources and try to prosper as a unity for the first time, having only recently parted from their Soviet mentors. Perhaps the vineyards along the road from Rijeka would thrive again, in this region known as vinodol.

Back in the car I unfolded my map. Unbelievably here was Novi, so there must be more to it than this hotel, when and if it became accessible.

The van driver came to look over my shoulder. I pointed to the forbidding track.

"Where does that track lead to? What name of village, town?"

"Gospič."

My finger traced this and that line on the map.

"Here, down here, on the right."

It did not seem very far at first glance. I tried calculating the kilometres. A hundred, and fifty, three hours?

"What! on that surface!" he laughed, but was still convinced the question was prompted by curiosity. Never for a moment believing I was contemplating it. I am not sure that I did just then. I was neutral.

He stepped aside to let me turn the car in the restricted space available. I switched on. Nothing happened. The engine was dead. I couldn't believe it! It had worked beautifully all the way from London. As the kindly van driver peered inside the bonnet, I remembered being warned in England: 'Never let anyone fiddle with this engine in Jugoslavia, they just wouldn't know' I searched at the back for a tool box. Nothing. Under the seats. Nothing. It had never occurred to me to check when buying the car. This was indeed a case of: 'An Innocent Abroad'. Perhaps in the glove compartment. Nothing, not even a screwdriver, and a screwdriver was just what was now needed. This man did know. He lengthened a connection and then started the engine with a screwdriver! He eyed me with wonder:

"Not even a screwdriver!" he slapped his hand on his thigh and laughed heartily, "across Europe with not even a screwdriver! *Peccato!* "

When I turned the car to face the wild track he must have held his breath unbelieving, then he called out:

"Do not let the engine stop on the way, it may not start again, without a screwdriver, and there is nothing, just nothing till you get to Gospič" then added: "and it is like this right to the top!"

CHAPTER 2

Gospič - Split

I had never, since my driving test, tackled anything but asphalted surfaces. As soon as the wheels hit this track of boulders and pot holes, my foot reached for the brake, my head hit the ceiling, the luggage tumbled about, the car bounced from side to side .I tightened my grip on the steering wheel. It was like trying to hold a team of wild horses.

I drove at a speed of five miles per hour, trying to miss the hole on the right only to hit the rock on the left. Stones everywhere. Big ones, too big to drive over. I swallowed hard. It was frightening. But how to turn back? No space. Not that I contemplated doing so! The shipping clerk's words were still in my ears: 'Buses do it, so can you.'

Mountain succeeded mountain... karst, a kind of limestone, porous pale grey. Nothing else. Desolate. Fortunately the sun shone and it was still early in the day. That unappetizing hotel in Rijeka had prompted me to leave without breakfast; now I was glad of the time gained. I nibbled a biscuit when daring to lift a hand from the wheel. AMO behaved gallantly through it all. As for me, inside the car, I was self contained, with all my bits and pieces, and at home wherever I went while the scenery passed by.

Suddenly we caught up with a stream of horse-drawn carts, peasants, in colourful costume, on foot, with huge loads on their heads. They waved, grinning broadly. But, when they realized I was by myself, they threw their caps in the air cheering: *"Jenska...Jenska!"*

The women's cheering was delirious, for one of their kind, driving alone, daring to...That night at the hotel, searching for, the ladies, I discovered the meaning of *'Jenska'*. There are divers ways of making one's education, and do not the French say: Les voyages forment la jeunesse... not necessarily only la jeunesse!

Could this be the remains of that road built in 1786 and named after Maria-Theresa? Who could tell me? Would anyone really believe I climbed up this impassable track? In retrospect I can hardly do so myself.

The three hours I had calculated for the climb had come and gone and there was still nothing but Karst. Where had all those people been heading for? There seemed nowhere to go. I wound up the window, it was getting colder up here. Of a sudden, mercifully, no more drop. We drove through a defile. A beehive-shaped hut of mud and twigs, stood atop on the right.

A ragged peasant woman carried a load of small wood on her back, a dirty cloth wrapped round her head and drawn across her mouth. She ignored me, indifferent to all but her own harsh life.

After sunset a fine drizzle set in and soon Gospič appeared through the mist. Being so tired, I never gave a thought to what might have happened had the drizzle come while I was climbing that rocky track. I had other more pressing things in mind.

Gospič, as far as I could make out in the gloom, was an assemblage of muddy lanes and dilapidated houses. Crawling uncertainly, looking for a garage to park AMO, I saw a young girl pushing a pram with luxurious trappings out of place in these squalid surroundings, with a blond baby in it. In halting English she implied there was no garage.

"Hotel?"

She shook her head, then beckoned me to follow her home. In these parts they spoke Serbo-Croat, one of the three languages used by the different nationalities that went to make up Jugoslavia, namely: Serbs, Croats, Slovens, Macedonians and Montenegrins. The other two spoken are Sloven and Macedonian. Two alphabets are in current use, the Latin around here and in Serbia Cyrillic, invented by St. Cyrill in the ninth century.

The square stone bungalow to which she led me appeared in better condition than most. Within however, it was a little hovel. A large room overheated by an enamel stove served as kitchen, living-room and bedroom. Fortunately there were no animals inside, as often happens.

The old grandmother, all in black, explained in Italian, that the girl was just back from a stay with an aunt in the United States hence the luxurious pram. As in the Middle East, affluence is largely a matter of public display, people are not house proud, not even in Greece, come to think of it, where a beautifully dressed woman might offer you coffee from a cup with no handle in a scruffy primitive kitchen.

They plied me with warm hospitality. Oven crisp bread, boiling milk with thick curds floating about.

There was no garage anywhere, confirmed the old woman, but they would keep my car in their garden. They could also put me up, there, she pointed to a corner of the floor space. The girl said they must first get permission from the 'Secretary' (of the Communist Party). Eventually they were persuaded to show me to the hotel, such as it was.

On the way there, I tried to convey to the girl that I wished to take her to dine somewhere. There was a lit up sign and noise coming from some premises. She kept pulling me by the sleeve and saying: "No, no." As we passed the door, I realised my mistake, the place was crammed with coarsely loud men drinking, amidst thick smoke. We fled.

I later learnt in London from a Jugoslav émigré, that Gospič had been a fashionable resort and its hotel one of the highlights. There was still some marble left on the ornamental staircase, with a grimy white statue holding a torch.

Behind the statue I found the conveniences. The one marked: 'jenska' was beyond possible use, next door 'maski' only slightly less repulsive. I now had two more words to my vocabulary, at a price!

There was no one about. Upstairs I found a long corridor of bare unscrubbed boards with doors on both sides. Then a head poked out from a hatch. The *Portir* was more like a prison warder, and German speaking. I said my piece learnt by heart?

"Yedna krevadna soba" - one room with one bed.

On receipt of my passport and the sum of 370 dinars (three shilling and six pence at the time) he gave me the key to a room.

There were six iron beds in the *yedna krevadna soba*, adorned with one grey blanket each. The young girl had helped me carry my Dunlopillo cushions to the door downstairs, I now placed them on top of the bed, the floor was barely fit for muddy boots, and spread my pale green sheets and rug over it.

After a while the *Portir* brought back my passport and a basin of boiling water gained with another of my prepared sentences: *Topla voda*. I was now able to wash, soak my frozen feet in it and quickly pour it into my hot water bottle to help warm the bed. The cold was intense. Whereas the Portir had a brazier in his cubby-hole, everywhere else it must have been below zero. My teeth chattered.

The blankets from all six beds helped, but they were so thin. I added pillows on top together with my clothes.

By dawn I was so cold I got up, dressed at speed, and left. A thick fog blanketed the sad little town. There was no one about. When the car heater had thawed me I stopped to plug in my little kettle for coffee.

As I started slicing the fog, out of nowhere there appeared a kind of landrover crammed with the city's young bucks. Black moustachioed and fierce looking, but with generous rows of white teeth showing in broad grins. The news must have gone round about the O N E tourist, a woman alone at that and as I always look far younger than my years, a girl perhaps, what a morsel to be had for the asking, or without it. When they realised I would escape they changed tactics and tried to ram us broadsides. That was nasty... very... and we only just managed to make our getaway. But not for long. Another pirate stood in wait a way off with a battered car in the middle of the track and doors open on both sides blocking the way.

He slithered up and said something about having trouble with his gums. I was sorry but was unable to offer any first aid medication other than Dettol, which somehow might not be the thing for inflamed gums. I learnt later that in Italian gome means tyres. When he leaned against the door and tried to put in his hand to unfasten it I stepped on the accelerator, climbed over the mud bank on the left, slid down in front of his vehicle and the chase was on.

At twenty miles an hour it was terrific. Head hitting ceiling, wheel wrenched, out of grasp by the shock, visibility about two yards in the fog. He finally gave up, but after I had missed the pass and was now heading for the summit of Mount Velebit altitude two thousand metres. The sun was beginning to rise. There was no fog up here.

Everything was grey karst, right down to Montenegro. Not a blade of grass anywhere, it was as though we were in a sheath of stone, then out, higher and into another sheath as narrow and bare as before. No birds. No sounds of any kind. It was a grandiose, awe inspiring sight - a moonscape. I must take a photograph of AMO, if only to convince myself, in years to come, that I had been here.

I ran up forward to get a dramatic picture when... in the lens, it seemed that AMO was imperceptibly moving backwards on the steep incline... I ran, as I never ran before or since, and grabbed the hand brake tighter, staring unbelievably at the immense drop down which he might have plunged, leaving me bereaved.

I never knew I could gallop at this pace since my back trouble! It goes to show! Suddenly the recollection of Novi made my heart thump. What would I do up here if the engine refused to start... without a screwdriver?

This dirt road, a mere mule track, meandering like an Italian pasta twist, with terrifying drop now on the outside, and sheer grey rock on the inside, was fairly smooth. No cart wheel ruts, no pot holes. Could it be that no one ever used it? For years... centuries perhaps. For whence would they come and where would they go?

Beyond the chasm, on the opposite side, quite close, another sheer wall of rock. I gave thanks for not suffering from claustrophobia. We climbed from one sheath of stone into another from eight in the morning to three in the afternoon. Then, finally the Velebit was left behind as we emerged on to a vast plateau. The fog returned, the scenery was of the Russian steppes. Cold, bleak, unforgettable.

There were flocks of sheep everywhere tended by young shepherdesses clad in what looked like thick felt jackets and straight black pinafores heavily embroidered in bright colours; red ribbons adorned the wool they were spinning, the first non grey things I had seen since the morning. Horse drawn four wheel carts, similar to droshkis went by further in the centre of the plateau, the drivers in skin coats and fur caps with flaps over their ears.

In this more welcoming entourage I was encouraged to stop and have a sandwich watched by donkeys. Then on and on through never ending steppes. A little lower down near a village I had a puncture. As I was trying to change the wheel, a peasant came along followed by two women bent double under loads of wood. They stopped. He ordered them to help me, which they did smilingly. The spare tyre was not too good but he conveyed it might last till Obrovač. Children crowded round and received with thrilled cries the Italian sugar almonds I fortunately still had, whilst my helpers were overwhelmed with the gift of 100 dinars (one shilling).

On our way once more. People waved all the way and called wishes. I smiling, bowing head to right and left feeling rather regal.

As dusk fell we came in sight of lovely Trogir down below us. It had once belonged to Byzantium, as had most of this coast. That is to say that theoretically it owed obedience to the Empire but never bothered to obey, and the Empire, for its part, had other more pressing matters to deal with. Still there could be Byzantine icons and frescoes to see.

The tiny city nestled on a little island reached only by a narrow bridge that looked very precarious. I recalled that warning never to venture upon a bridge not indicated on my route sheet, for it might be rotten in the centre. This one was not mentioned. Perhaps I had enough adventures for one day. I better not risk AMO on a collapsible way. Oh well next time... However this 'next time' business seldom comes ones way, and so I missed seeing Trogir, with its history of Venetian, Austrian and French occupation and its superb architectural treasures.

The Island of Čiovo, across the water, began to light up, somewhat rheumatically. There was little electric power yet in the country at that time.

Along the coast road now we encountered sailors, and Naval Depots. Rather untidy, like scrap yards it seemed in the half light. Above us I fancied the shadows of castles built centuries ago as defences against the Turks.

Since those early 'after the war' days, an Autoput was made to bypass this coast road, it lead to new tourist resorts and luxury hotels. By 1964/65, the road from Rijeka to Split was mostly finished and by 1968 it went along the Makarska Riviera as far as Brela, in Vrula Bay, and the luxury Hotel Maestro. I am glad though, my first visit was on to that promontory, precarious and rough as it was, but so beautiful, peaceful, lonely, everything life in the West has now lost. First impressions are so important, like seeing San Marco in Venice for the first time from under the colonnade at the far end of the Piazza. But, being able to drive from Rijeka to Dubrovnik on a made coast road seemed a miracle, to one who had to meander inland on stony tracks and climb the two thousand metres up Velebit to reach Split.

This dirt road followed the indentations of the coast. Then, suddenly a blaze of lights, such as I had not seen since Italy, Split at last. The streets were crowded with people, there was no traffic; groups of gesticulating men talking, laughing even. The ban against gatherings had been lifted a mere forty eight hours earlier. 'Big brother' seemed well and truly dropped. Tito had broken with the yoke of the USSR. However many of its dictates remained. Near the waterfront a concrete building all painted red with an enormous illuminated yellow hammer and sickle over its frontage splashed the message it stood for to the new Jugoslavia. Next to it a minute baroque Catholic church nestled shyly; while a little further on an attractive arched quadrangle with steps led to the port on the other side.

Putnik garage was quite a way off. It was strictly for lorries and buses. There was no other traffic anyway, we had always been the only car. AMO would have to spend a lonely night amidst these giants. A young mechanic, Belgian born and bred, who had settled here with his family since 1947, did his best to accommodate us.

Walking to the hotel through narrow alleyways reminiscent of Genoa, I emerged on to a small piazza packed with men talking animatedly, letting off steam after so many years of repression. A jewel of a little piazza out of a musical comedy, with seventeenth century stone balconies and lovely Italian windows obviously of the Venetian era. I learnt later that all this architecture was the work of local genius inspired by Venice. At the opposite corner rose a Medieval castello with a tower, and in the centre of the piazza the statue of a local poet. It was a lovely warm night, and it was November!

The Hotel Bellevue was quite comfortable in spite of the smell of drains everywhere, including my room. The main thing I remember about this hotel was forgetting my new roll of paper in the loo. In the dining-room were a few well dressed couples of the intelligentsia with a decidedly Komrad Doktor atmosphere.

Next morning being Sunday, I went back to the little Catholic church beside the H.Q. of the Communist Party. The sun shone upon these incongruously coupled buildings and I unslung my Rolleiflex. What a picture for a London Newspaper! When suddenly, on the previously empty piazza a man appeared, loitering. Long overcoat as usual, soft hat, I put back my camera. It would be a pity to be arrested so soon, as Robert Adam had been two centuries ago when making his sketches of Diocletian's Palace, which gave us that elegant style.

Inside the church, through clouds of incense, four or five locals made up the congregation. At the altar the priest appeared through the haze, wearing elaborate vestments of green and gold and a high gold mitre. The language was strange. Not Latin. After a while, a Frenchman in front of me leaned towards his local companion:

"Ça ce n'est pas catholique. Je m'en vais."

I followed them to the cathedral situated within the mausoleum of Diocletian. It was octagonal, in white marble, raised upon a pedestal reached by marble steps. A heavy sheet of leather, now drawn to one side, masked the entrance. Where could the carved wood doors be? Perhaps still stored for the duration of the war? They were part of the Christian church made by a local artist in the thirteenth century. These people really carved superbly, as the pulpit within showed, though a trifle heavy. The interior of this building was round. I was struck by the fact that this pagan historic monument had not been deprived of its character through its conversion to the Christian faith.

However here too Mass was said in Croatian, a rite recognised by Rome as is also that of the Armenian church. Gregur Ninski, whose gigantic statue by Mestrovič stood near the golden gate, was largely instrumental, in the tenth century, for retaining the Croatian rite. Under the photograph given to me by Putnik Tourist Office that morning, he was styled: Saint Gregory. They also gave me a great deal of other pictures and literature. I was apparently the only tourist. The Frenchman seemed to be here on business. Mestrovič's own likeness in bronze was also enormous on another picture, like Michelangelo in old age. He was undoubtedly "the" Jugoslav sculptor, and his work is scattered throughout the country and as far out of it as Israel.

Coming out of the Cathedral what a sight! In the bright sunshine a large expanse of marble with the Palace of Diocletian stretching right and left and across. A black-clad peasant woman surrounded with large shallow baskets overflowing with flowers, under a blue and red striped umbrella, made a vivid splash of colour in the centre of the marble peristyle with the South entrance to the private apartments of the palace at the back. A double colonnade leads to a Grecian - but here arched - fore-front surmounted by a Grecian pediment.

You have to use your imagination to visualise what it could have been like when built for it covers nearly ten acres and in the course of centuries has suffered all sorts of unimaginable devastation. There are houses everywhere within its walls, even to a factory making the Dalmatic, a loose tunic with slit sleeves and sides worn to this day by ecclesiastics.

When it was built this whole area was known as Spalato - from the Greek: *sto palati* - to the palace - which is quite probable as it took ten years to build by presumably Greek architects and masons who would refer to it thus. There had been Greek settlements on this spot for centuries.

Other instances of such play on words are Istanbul, which is meant to derive from the Greek: *is stin poli* - to the city, Constantinopoli - which until not so long ago was referred to in Greek as just: *'stin poli'* to the city - a custom of centuries when speaking of the most magnificent capital of the known world.

Diocletian, after a year's illness spent in his palace at Nicomedia - his capital of the East, across the water from Byzantium - retired to his native Illyria. He was fifty nine. His co-Emperor Maximian, had to abdicate too, in accordance with the pledge taken at his investiture. It is extraordinary to read about all these gentlemanly agreements, and more incredible that they were actually observed, bearing in mind the murders, poisonings, double crossings and miscellaneous horrors perpetrated by their predecessors! One marvels at the force of character of this son of a freedman of Illyria - not a shepherd as happened later - who managed to raise himself to this rank. As Gibbon puts it: 'The arduous work of rescuing the distressed empire from tyrants and barbarians had been completely achieved by a succession of Illyrian peasants'. For Maximian was also from Dalmatia as were many others.

And so it seems fitting that a man such as Diocletian should have built for himself the most magnificent palace in Europe. Even to this day, bearing in mind what it must have been, it is beyond compare, with its Grecian elegance and purity of line.

It was all blocked up with rubble, and peopled by what I took to be squatters, but realised in time that they had lived within those walls for centuries, as they do in Constantinople's land walls. In Italy too, such people have taken quarters in palaces. I remembered in Ferrara seeing strings of colourful washing along the exquisite loggia, mingling with the frescoes of the ceiling, and then children pouring out of the palace, within which a school was housed. It takes time to get used to that kind of thing.

I stepped upon the large square slabs of white marble worn down to a mellow pale honey by the centuries. Did Diocletian walk on this very stone? Or was he forever carried aloft having deified himself in good time to inspire awe and added safety from a murderer's dagger. Can a living god stoop to walking? Who can tell!

I had a friend from London to see here, Jocelyn, trained with the then Saddlers Wells Ballet, who had a year's engagement with the Jugoslav State Ballet. I found her residing in ex-King Peter's summer villa set in idyllic surroundings on a rock jutting out to sea, with magnificent scenery on all sides. Had I been here but a few weeks earlier I would have seen a unique spectacle of the ballet in the marble peristyle in front of Diocletian's Palace! She also danced in the house of the sculptor Mestrovič, which he had donated to the state. It was situated in woodland on the outskirts of Split on the lower slopes of Mount Marion. Here too with grand views towards town and sea beyond. It was used for cultural events. Later it became the Maritime Museum.

Jocelyn was sorry I had missed a visit to Trogir. The bridge, she told me, was sound enough to bear an old London Transport bus, in which she was driven there. Such buses were still in use, sent over after the war as help to the Jugoslavs.

To think that if AMO and I had embarked on that ferry from Rijeka I would have missed seeing all this! A warm thought for the Rijeka 'Feminist"!

CHAPTER 3

Dubrovnik

Split to Dubrovnik by road, 250 kilometres on the Autoput, was child's play. In 1957 there was only that dirt road hugging the coast and it was beautiful, but slow and bumpy. Being the only road user in the twentieth century is quite an experience!

Olive groves sloped down the red earth to the sea, tiny villages perched on the edge of the cliff like clusters of semi-precious stones; the road narrowing still more at these points, we often followed the wider way and found ourselves ending up by the shore, amidst a fishing community. Krilo was one of these. As I drove up men were playing bowls over the surface of the road. There were shrieks of dismay and incredulity as emerging round the corner I tried to miss the bowls but still hit one. Never mind, broad grins, waves and good wishes. Everywhere people were so pleasant.

The mileage, occasionally indicated, was hazy, 60 kilometres to the next locality soon became 70. The scenery was breathtaking all the way. The main islands Brač, Hvar, and many smaller ones scattering the emerald sea, kept us company for quite a way. The sun beat down on rock of varying shades of red and green; Sometimes a light haze drifting upon the water added a fairy tale quality to the scene.

Vineyards thrive all along this coast where Greek settlements existed long before Alexander the Great. No buildings of any kind interfered with the natural splendour of nature, apart form the ancient stone houses closely packed in the villages.

Poultry behaved hysterically, scattering in disarray at our approach, cockrels in panic flew on to the roof of the car atop the luggage, screaming their heads off, until I stopped to let them fly down.

We went through Omiš, larger than most, later a sea-side resort. By the time we got to Gradač, I began to wonder whether Dubrovnik could be reached before nightfall.

After straying down to the seashore for the second time, I took a picture of Maraška, stretching lazily out to sea on its high rocky promontory. A kindly lorry driver advised me to follow him to a tiny village where there was a hotel. On the way we met a Capuchin monk who thought the hotel in question was all right. As darkness fell we came within sight of a dimly lit square construction from which issued a din of wailing gramophone music together with a crescendo of men's voices. The innkeeper, bottle and glass in hand, stood riveted to the ground on seeing us, while his patrons rushed out, not wishing to miss such an extraordinary diversion. Children running from the other end of the village hemmed us in. I backed the car, trying to miss as many of the human obstacles as possible, and beat a hasty retreat.

Next we tried Metković, which looked bigger on the map, but to reach it we had to negotiate the marshes on the estuary of the Neretva, driving on narrow criss-cross causeways. Tall dark mountains towered close above. Often, when finding no exit from a causeway, we had to reverse on the narrow strip trying not to fall in the water surrounding us. The moon helped but could be deceptive. There were barracks and depots all the way on dry land and sailors everywhere. Since those days the marshes on the Neretva were reclaimed for agriculture.

At Metković, the hotel could vie with that of Gospić for lack of luxury. The anaemic lighting, certainly not more than 10 watt bulbs, helped to shroud the general sleaziness, but the Portir turned out to be unusual in that he spoke French, learnt at school, and seemed better educated than most seen so far, though wearing the usual collarless open neck shirt and drab clothes.

He showed me to a room, with unbelievably, one bed only, which could just about be discerned in the dim light. It cost 300 dinars (3 shillings). He could not understand why I needed a jug of hot water, and was afraid it might crack the ewer standing in the basin. However when it came, in an enamel jug, the water was very hot though smelling of lard.

When I needed to brush a tooth, I spotted a tap at the end of a two foot pipe sticking from the floor boards on the landing, with enamel basin under it. The very thing!

The hotel seemed to be full of comrades, but by the time I entered the restaurant it was empty. They had only come for a drink after all. Not trusting the water I asked for tea, brought in a thick cup already served and sweetened, the colour of champagne and tasting of lard. Dinner was 200 dinars and not at all bad.

At about 10 p.m. I was awakened by an awful din under the paper thin bedroom floor. A band! A real band!... Could these labourers be wanting to dance? But there were never any women about in public places. Anyway for the next few hours sleep was out of the question.

Breakfast the next morning in the restaurant was 100 dinars. When I asked for a second cup of tea the serving man nearly choked at the extravagance.

By daylight this looked a sad uninteresting valley, no use even trying to get petrol, what would they need it for, nothing motorised in sight. As I kicked the tyres pondering, two young men leapt from a lorry just driving in, with pump; refusing money they wished us: *"buon viaggio."*

Soon we rejoined the coast, which was even lovelier than before, and by late morning we stopped on the edge of a promontory with a view over a tiny monastery perched upon a rock jutting out to sea. Yet another scene to make you wish to linger. I made Nescafé and had lunch.

We reached Dubrovnik soon after eleven; Putnik Office outside the town gate arranged for garaging AMO and gave all the information for the next stage of the drive. They said it was impossible to reach Peč in one day, even thought it was only 204 kilometres. A night must be spent at Kotor, and another at Titograd. I did not like the idea.

I entered Ragusa - Dubrovnik, at the wrong time of day, according to Rebecca West, for the light was not: 'just faintly blue with dusk in the open space that lies inside the gate' ... but mid day and the sun streamed in warming the mellow stone.

As I stepped on the drawbridge over the moat, a tall woman of proud bearing, was coming out, in a magnificent costume with an enormous halo-like coif of white organdi, and she let me take a picture, my best of the entire trip. She gave me her address and I promised to send her a print.

As you entered the town you caught your breath, for it looked like a jewel set on a polished white plate. I stood and gazed at it all for quite a while before taking in the architectural detail.

The monument to catch the eye was of course the large domed fifteenth century fountain by the Neapolitan Onofrio della Cava. It was the most massive of its kind I had ever seen, with 14 jets of water sprouting from lions' mouths in the centre of delicately chiselled foliage, between colonnettes with tiny pediments. The water was contained in a basin that ran round the domed structure. What with the church of St. Saviour standing so near to it, it reminded me of a fountain for ablutions in front of a mosque.

But there was so much to admire too soon. Next door to the oldest apothecary in the world, probably dating from 1317, with its very modern equivalent dispensing near by, was the Franciscan Monastery of about the same period, with the loveliest compact and elegant cloister imaginable, running round a green quadrangle with a fountain in the centre. The dainty arches were supported by slender columns with varied capitals of figures and foliage.

As you walked along the Corso over the square slabs of white marble, you realised each building was a masterpiece of exquisite proportions. Beyond, rose the massive fortification walls that saved this unique town, city State, Republic, from many a threat to its sovereignty. It was not until ten years after my first visit that the town was finally cleaned and spruced up for the budding tourist trade; that November 1957 I did not see another tourist.

These walls were formidable and wide. The view from up there, over sea and islands to one side and on the other overlooking the town with, beyond it, gardens, villas right up the mountain slopes, had to be seen to be believed, it was absolutely lovely.

This jewel of a city was of course reminiscent of Venice, in miniature. A republic, a city state, a perfect work of art. The Rector here as the Doge there was elected by a council, but here for a short period. The system was carried to extremes, for fear of a dictatorship, which happened twice in the course of their history. The Rector was elected for one month only and more or less incarcerated in his palace, emerging only for festivals and state occasions, richly clad in a red robe with a stole of black velvet over his left shoulder. He was followed by his special guard, and preceded by musicians!

Though to be elected must have been a tremendous achievement, it was as well that the period was short, else the man subjected to such close scrutiny and suspicion might have gone round the bend.

The Palace in which each Rector bore his honorific burden was another work of art, perhaps the greatest in the country, by the Florentine Michelozzo-Michelozzi, most of it anyway, and certainly the exquisitely proportioned Renaissance loggia, its arches supported by elegant columns with composite capitals, all different. Michelozzi had built the Medici Palazzo in Florence and the villas, also churches and many other works of distinction.

So much artistic achievement concentrated in a restricted space was overwhelming. You were about to turn right under the loggia, into the courtyard of the Rector's Palace when your eye was caught by the Sponza Palace, another beautiful work, against a backcloth of mountains, their lower slopes dotted with villas.

Within that courtyard a narrow stone staircase lead up to the state rooms housing a history museum. A slight white haired woman hailed me in French from the top of the stairs. She was, she said the historian writing under the name of 'Natalie de Raguse', had I not read her latest book: 'Raguse Etape Royale'?

She advised a stay at the Hotel Dubravka, an old patrician mansion and the only hotel within the old town, run by the owners:

"Well, they let them run it, you know, that's a way of being allowed to live in their own home I suppose".

She seemed intent to take me in hand and show me everything, but cooled off upon hearing I meant to stay only one day.

The hotel was indeed a Patrician home. My room overlooked a lovely terrace with the mansion's private chapel. The embroidered bed linen must have been their family's own. The cost of the room 4 shillings, dinner was 2/6 served with refinement by pretty girls in black dresses with starched white aprons and head pieces, obviously the parlour-maid outfit of past times. Tables were covered in starched damask.

When I tried to question one serving girl about the history of the house, she referred me to the young woman supervising from a desk, implying she was one of the owners of the stately home; but when paying my bill I asked, her face took on a stony expression and she said evasively:

"It is a hotel as any other, that is all."

It was a balmy evening. After dinner I strolled in the smooth paved streets, free of traffic, as in Venice. Here however, the town was built up on various levels reached by narrow stone steps and alleyways. Houses had balconies, gardens and carved portals, sometimes packed close yet on the whole giving the impression of space. Airy. The people here were very good looking, courteous and attentive, more individualistic, not so much of the comrade stuff. It still was a patrician city in spite of present circumstances.

Since those days, new hotels were built outside the city, some first class, but there was a choice for every purse. Many shops appeared within the old town, selling all sorts of things, not necessarily enhancing the tone of the place, which used to be of dignified sobriety.

By 1958 you could fly from Belgrade in an unpressurized plane. There was, however, no air strip at Dubrovnik but the plane managed to land somehow. Within nine years there was an airport.

I walked right round once more, to take another look at the cathedral rebuilt after the terrific earthquake of 1667, which demolished the town and decimated the population. By an extraordinary freak of destiny a statue of St. Blaise, the patron saint of the city, escaped destruction in the baroque church opposite the Rector's Palace. The saint held a silver replica of the town as it was before the catastrophe, which must have been even more beautiful than at present. The cathedral shown on this tablet was that built supposedly by Richard-Coeur-de-Lion in thanksgiving for escaping shipwreck on this coast. But what of that other story whereby Richard was captured on the island of Lokrum, and incarcerated in an Austrian citadel at Dürnstein? and was it not the money paid for his ransom that helped to build that cathedral and also shore up the walls of Vienna?

The following day I kept postponing my departure, as when I need to tear myself away from Venice, carrying my bag along the Piazzetta, stopping for a last cappuccino, an excuse for a prolonged farewell before bringing myself to take the vaporetto to my car. Here the car was but a few yards away outside the gate of the city. I must go, but I would return. However this first visit could never be matched for I had the entire place to myself.

CHAPTER 4

Kotor - Peč

Leaving lovely Dubrovnik regretfully I rejoined AMO and hit the coast road towards Kotor. The scenery was Arcadian in its beauty as far as Caftat: pronounced "Saftat", which was within twenty kilometres. From the seaward side it must be even lovelier and without the cares of driving over uneven ground. By 1967 you could stay at the Hotel Caftat, modest but good. There was even a night-club where Brandy for six came to under £2.

After a while it became rather monotonous, a military area to all appearances but for the absence of soldiers. Notices - a sketch of a red X across a camera - forbade the taking of photographs. Later, when rounding one of the endless zigzags on the narrow road, a white cottage appeared with a large letter box - a small post office. As I dropped in the cards left unposted, the Postmaster, in shirt sleeves, sunning himself at an upstairs window, called out in Italian that my letters would get quicker to their destination if posted from Titograd. He came down, unlocked the box and handed them back to me. These people were so naturally kind and friendly.

At Perašt the Naval presence made itself felt. There were sailors everywhere and Naval depots. Perašt was named after Peter the Great of Russia, who sent young recruits here to train at the Naval College, famed for discipline.

No one had heard of a ferry to take us across La Bocca di Cattaro, as Putnik had claimed. At the Tourist Office, a kind man with faultless French, learnt at The Friars College in Constantinople, was close to tears with emotion on hearing I was on my way there. I later sent him a picture postcard from his beloved city.

Driving now, for lack of a ferry, round La Bocca - The Gulf of Kotor - the road sagged to sea level and I dropped to a snails pace for fear the engine might take in sea water. Once again the view was worth the hardships of the drive. To the left strips of small townships with beautiful Venetian palaces dwarfed by forbidding bare karst mountains. On a sunless day it must look grim. Even now barely at noon, it was beginning to recede into gloom, for this range rose Westward.

The sea view was extraordinary, an intricate fjord with wide bays. In the furthermost black rocks stood sentinel well out to sea. It was beautiful in a fantastic way.

The Hotel Slavja in Kotor, indicated by Putnik, overlooked the sea. With so much sea water around I looked forward to a fresh fish lunch. It was primitive as hotels go, and in comparison to what is there now, but it was run as a catering school by enthusiastic students anxious to please. In the 1980s you could not help marvelling at the steady if slow, efforts made to promote the tourism of the future, which became one of Jugoslavia's main foreign trades. These young people, of peasant stock, in whose villages life had stood still for centuries, had to be taught everything from scratch. The excellence of staff being a major factor in the success of a hotel, they had much to learn if the establishment they would run could hope to reach western European standards. In the winter months, when most hotels closed the staff went back to their villages to other work but schools existed in some of these places where they could learn languages, and perfect themselves in the art of catering.

There was clean, if rough linen on the bed and student parlour maids in neat uniform. Most of the students spoke French, they crowded round my table eager to tell me all they knew of the region's history, which they still called 'Cattaro'. They told of invasions starting with the Romans, ending with the Russians and English. Of a terrible earthquake - probably the very same that destroyed Ragusa in the seventeenth century - they had others, since my first visit, the worst in 1979 after which much rebuilding was undertaken. They insisted I must see the 12th century Cathedral, if only from the outside, for it was closed. Here there were Orthodox churches as well as Catholic, the two communities living in harmony side by side.

The fish, when they brought it to me was skeletal, under a thick camouflage of tomato sauce. It glared at me with a haggard eye, daring me to eat it. There was a little flesh with the bones.

The male students were very interested in AMO which I let them inspect. Thrilled to peer inside the bonnet and sit behind the wheel. Had they never seen a car at such close quarters before? It is true we had met with no other on the roads. By 1963 a few small Jugoslav cars made by Fiat, appeared on the highways, under the name of FICA. (meaning small in Serbo-Croat) Soon after, Traffic Police patrolled near petrol stations stopping anyone who failed to slow down. As there were no warning signs you were an easy prey, and having to pay a fine on the spot, you could not help wondering who pocketed the money. A FIAT Plant had been inaugurated at Kragujevač in 1962 and later Jugo-cars were made there under licence from Fiat, but it took until 1980 for the first of these to be put on the roads. By 1985, however, they were being exported to the United States, the lure being the price which was low by comparison to any produced elsewhere. Labour was excessively cheap in Jugoslavia where a worker in such a factory could not hope to get more than £60 to £80 per month, in spite of the cost of living going up to nearly that in the West. Bread was only slightly cheaper than in Britain and there were bread queues. Meat was scarce and expensive, but transport was cheap.

The tourist was not affected as the exchange rate was still very much in his favour, but for the local population it was a hard life. Those who could went to work in Germany (about seven hundred thousand of them) where they earned more realistic wages. The others made do as best they could, I was reminded of that chap who tried to do away with me and pinch the car in 1957. Not much seemed to have changed in 30 years. He had told me he earned about six pence per hour.

While in Kotor in 1957, I went to explore the alleyways and tiny piazzas of the mediaeval little town from which, soon after lunch, the sun was already beginning to retreat behind the mountains towering over it. From a distance, hugging the bare stone, it looked like a bas-relief upon the rock-face. Yet is had been a thriving centre once, for it was on the trade route to Constantinople. But I definitely would not choose to stay here, in spite of the fantastic grandeur of the views both seaward and up the Lovčen.

At breakfast the following morning, the students were awe struck when they heard I was heading for Cetinje - they pronounced it Tsetinje. Taking me outside with my slice of bread in hand, they pointed up the bare vertical peak:

"Look up there, you cannot climb Skaljari, the road is terrible, can you see that bare ribbon twisting up and up? That is Skaljari."

At first sight I could see nothing remotely resembling a road on the bare karst face of the mountain, but then I did, well yes, it was rather on the vertical side, so narrow.

"Crna-Gora, Montenegro, the Black Mountain" they whispered, "you cannot go up Skaljari in a car, how could you, it is almost vertical. It is vertical."

Lovčen was nearly two thousand metres, they insisted, well so was Velebit, perhaps more, I wasn't quite sure. Though I had researched about the art treasures to see on this trip, I had not given much thought to such pedestrian matters as the state of roads, possible mountains barring the way or their altitude. The only height on the route known to me for certain was the 'Grande Corniche' from Nice, in the South of France, for which I thought I had trained, driving on the highest ridge of the Chilterns near my home. Now however, after what I had gone through, the 'Grande Corniche' recalled a polished ballroom floor.

When they realised this route was on my A.A. sheet and I was bent on going on they did their best to hurry me on, worrying lest the weather changed - though the sun shone with not a cloud in the sky.

"Ah but it can change, by the time you arrive at the top, and when there is a thunderstorm it is frightful, you just cannot possibly know what it can be. Impossible to stay up there during a storm."

The thunderclaps, they said, were thrown from peak to rock face back and forth, and it was terrifying. They did their best to turn me into a nervous wreck. I couldn't go back the way I came. Anything would be better than that. Not knowing the evil ahead was less daunting than the other way round somehow. It couldn't be worse than Velebit.

It wasn't. For fearful though it looked from below, it was a quicker climb, being almost vertical. Twisting in the sharpest hair-pin bends and again before you could recover from the previous one. It was too steep to stop for a photograph, and we might not be able to start again on this incline. Still I managed to catch hasty glimpses of the view below between bends. Kotor far away, as a handful of small pebbles with the black sentinel rocks looking no bigger than coffee beans. As I went up they rapidly receded to the size of specks. The climb being so abrupt I felt the rareness of the air, but mercifully not the sickness as when going up Velebit, which might have been caused then by the lack of breakfast. Now it was like being at the top of a Karst needle or looking down from another planet. Rather exhilarating!

When we reached the summit it was not clear whether this was indeed Lovčen Pass, for it was not at all as mountain passes were expected to be. Instead, a small village huddled there Njguši, where the Prince-Bishop and poet of Montenegro Petar II, known as Njegoš, the students had said, was born in 1813. His enormous mausoleum was at the top with a gigantic black marble statue by Mestrovič.

We reached a vast bleak plateau where peasant women in black felt costume richly embroidered in bright colours, tended flocks of sheep. My expectations of a rapid descent were dashed, for the road on the far side of the plateau led even higher, to another mountain, a pass and again a mountain. There hadn't been any boulders on this climb, perhaps the steepness of it made them roll down with the winter rains that must be torrential. All in all the fears of the students were probably justified. It must be like a nightmare up here in a storm. The sun was shining now, but it was bitterly cold and windy, I looked forward to the descent towards Cetinje, only to find it was only slightly less high, but as cold and as windy.

Had it been alive instead of like an empty shell I would have imagined moving along the stage of a musical comedy about Ruritania, however as it was I had the decor to myself. Where were the actors? In the fields? The fields, such as could be seen were patches of earth amidst the karst. How could anyone live in such conditions? These people claimed to have once belonged to the plains of Serbia, why didn't they go back, one wondered? These were a cluster of houses in the middle of mounds and peaks of pumice-stone.

The Prince-Bishop's Palace, a square house painted almond green with a frieze running round under the roof like a Wedgwood vase, with two white columns on either side of the front door surmounted by a Grecian Pediment, did its best, which wasn't much. Its shutters were of plain wood, like those of cottages, without laths.

Njegoš, the Prince-Bishop and poet, an extraordinary character, renowned for his learning and eccentricity, had a billiard table carried up all the way from Kotor, along the mule-track. It was a marvel to all and since that time the Palace is referred to as *'Biljarda'*.

The Hotel Grand, where Putnik had wanted me to spend another night, was reminiscent of that in Gospič, but also deserted. Not even a cat in the streets, or rather piazzas. The ground was of earth. Finally I found some people. They were a different type, tall, proud and fierce looking. Montenegrins, and they referred to their country not as

Jugoslavia, nor Cetinje but Montenegro, always. After all Jugoslavia as an entity was very recent. Montenegro was renowned for its fighters throughout the centuries, and its... brigands, but Montenegrins might not see themselves in that light for in their heart there was the ideal brigand, somewhat like Robin Hood.

Cetinje, this rugged wild capital of Montenegro could have been lovely given a spark of life. Its people were kindly and deplored the fact they had no petrol to offer. I went on my way. The scenery was breathtaking cold and fearsome. Black mountains towered above, deep black canyons below. Suddenly half way down one of the canyons an incredibly narrow parapetless bridge astride a turbulent stream sandwiched between two high mountains and a man on a donkey crossing leisurely. He was draped in a flowing mantle and wide brimmed black hat, a living pen and ink drawing by Goya. It was impossible to stop for a picture, the dirt road was too narrow and twisting.

Further on, peasants were coming up clad in goat skins, driving a few oxen and sheep, and carrying wood. Mountain people, very poor but proud and fierce, now all smiles, calling greetings.

After a continuous scenery of black arid mountains I looked forward to reaching Titograd, a modern town with, presumably, all the comforts of which I had been deprived since leaving Italy. The way they all spoke of it made it sound like the city of cities. Bearing such a name! They must be very proud of it. It had been built over the ruins of Podgorica razed to the ground during the second world war. At last we descended into a vast empty plain. On the far side a cluster of little houses, all that was left of the old town. Elsewhere one or two wide streets and a park of the future. Large cubic buildings one of which was the Crna-Gora Hotel, and one other of the barrack category in a side street. Many policemen and a one way traffic system all for us! - though I spotted up to ten stationary cars; never seen so many since Trieste.

The chimneys of factories were close by, sometimes regretfully in pretty villages, and were welcomed as a sign of the progress of which the people were proud. The town looked under construction, not much of it yet, a mere project, it was obviously intended to have wide open spaces, which could be afforded as there was an immense flat plain all round it. At that moment however, it looked like a large tray holding two or three big tea pots but only two cups and no saucers.

There was no garage in the whole of Titograd, AMO could stay in front of the hotel, the night porter would keep an eye. The Crna-Gora was made of the stuff of luxury hotels but without the style of a truly 'Grand Hotel'. When my young friends of the Kotor catering school came of age it would no doubt, change for the better.

One of the two lifts took me to my room along wide thickly carpeted corridors. A double bedroom en suite, no single ones. The whole of my Chelsea flat could easily have been contained in it. Two telephones by the beds with beautiful woolly plaid blankets but skimpy sheets of rough material reaching neither the length nor breadth of the bed. I soaked for nearly an hour in the hot bath. The water, from an individual immersion heater, was boiling; but an open grating on the floor, which I hastily covered with a towel, gurgled with the waste water. I was to meet this system again throughout Turkey, as here, with no plugs to the basins and smells to boot! The cost of this room was 1.400 dinars, a real disaster to my finances. By contrast dinner was only 300 dinars.

Breakfast in the bedroom, what luxury! But what a waste of time, for it did not all come together and I had to ring many times for items such as butter, sugar, cup etc. brought singly with each call.

I left before eight, it was very cold. The one petrol station with a single pump for petrol and one for NAFTA, was already overtaken by 3 lorries and the ten cars spotted the night before. It was slow going. I decided to check the tyres only, but there was no machine. Driving on an empty road as directed, I found a yard with lorries under repair. No, they did not have a 'vulkanizer': try further on. In the end I gave up, it was by then 9.30 and there were 110 miles or so ahead of me. By then, with experience, I feared not to reach Peč before dark. Still, no more mountains, only a huge plain. My route sheet stated: 'mountainous country' but did not mention any high pass. After a while I began to worry about not taking petrol, but was told by a kindly bus driver I would find a petrol pump at Andrievica, about 90 kilometres away.

It became now less flat than Titograd; moderately mountainous, wild scenery. Andrievica, just a village with 2 pumps, one for petrol, seemed deserted. A man walked up lazily, no petrol he said, "Finito..." I insisted:

"Nije," he shrugged his shoulders, and retreated under cover again. He just could not care less. I had not met this type of man in

Jugoslavia before. As I drove away, the kindly bus driver arrived at the other pump. He called to insist for petrol. But my chap wouldn't even listen:

"Finito..." and he walked away again.

I would have to try at the next locality, not suspecting then that this was the last petrol pump before Peč. The bus driver, busy turning into position called again pointing to the pump, but what was the use if there was none.

I went on. After all I still had a can with ten litres. Coming out of a narrow gorge, suddenly, the scenery changed completely. We were surrounded by beautiful high mountains covered with trees. It was difficult to make out which way my next horizon might be for the road ahead vanished behind a hill. The highest and most luxuriant mountain rose far out of my way to the East, topping above a cloud. Yet I could distinctly make out the heads of trees covering it up to the summit; they looked woolly, cloud probably.

We had been gradually climbing for some time and must be quite high, the peak to the East must be Mount Čakor. After a narrow defile we climbed higher still. Now the woolly summit was left behind, but rounding the next hill I was at its base and climbing towards it. The ascent was easy, the road wider than usual and not so very stony nor gutted. Or perhaps I was getting used to hardship. All is relative after all. Soon we met with the trees, which were not shrouded in cloud but covered with snow. There were telegraph wires even up here, thick with frozen snow, like skeins of white wool. But the soil remained greenish yellow and brown. The contrast was stunning. As we went higher, the tall trees, the leafy kind, not firs, seemed to climb with us, as to a meeting at the top, the wind pushed their growth that way, and made them seem to move upwards to a gathering up there. Some dishevelled, from hurrying in the wind that had lashed them for years. I wondered whether the altitude had addled my wits but these trees looked alive.

At the summit, which was rounded, comfortable with plenty of space, I stopped to take pictures and have lunch. Any excuse to remain longer up in this fairy land. No noise, no wind, no animals, no birds, just the trees. A gurgling mountain stream tinkled out of a rock. Occasionally a packet of snow gathered speed and rushed from higher up to break in a myriad crystals on the road. A sudden 'splush' as snow fell from an overladen branch. I could not make up my mind to begin the descent and walked about, cup of coffee in hand. A military jeep came up from the opposite direction. I tried to find out in Italian what the weather conditions were like below, for there seemed to be a kind of dark fog. I thought they were interested in my photo taking. They got out of their vehicle and said many things animatedly, gesturing towards the thickness of the trees, and whence they had come, but it was in Serbo-Croat with a few words of Italian. French - speaking Jugoslavs met later, suggested they were probably warning against bear and wolf.

I eventually began the descent lost in rapture. Stopping to take close-ups of the trees, but suddenly it began to snow, or rather we had entered the snowing area, and before long we were in a thick blizzard. Perhaps that was what the military were trying to say? The blizzard became fiercer as we went. Snow piled up and froze on the windscreen. It was getting rapidly darker though only 3 in the afternoon. Then suddenly it was night. The snow covered the road and got inside the car through loose joints, after what poor AMO had suffered on bumpy roads. It seemed one tyre was a bit flat. Getting out to investigate with a torch, I fell flat on my face. The road was icy. I did have chains but had no idea how to fit them on. In the dark, freezing conditions it was a hopeless undertaking. Snow driven by icy wind got inside my clothes, eyes, ears. I got back in the car and carefully crawled along. The descent was much steeper, with sharp hair-pin bends. AMO kept losing grip and skidding, I knew there was a gaping drop on the outside.

It was so cold. The heater did not give much heat, no doubt on account of the slow motion. Then suddenly the petrol gave out. I had already used my ten litres. I found, in the course of this drive, how easy it was to die of cold. I was frozen and so sleepy suddenly. Huddling into a ball I was about to let myself fall asleep, when a blazing light against the windscreen roused me. A lorry... coming up! I slipped out and fell sitting on the ice, waving arms above my head.

Two young men jumped out and dashed to pick me up. They had no spare petrol, but as luck would have it, their engine worked on petrol, not NAFTA.
I pleaded:

"Prego... prego..."

One took my can while the other pumped petrol into a funnel which he stopped with his finger, and back and forth decanted the juice into my can.

A light from the rear. The friendly bus just catching up. Why oh why didn't I listen to him and insist on petrol at Andrievica? There was petrol, he knew; that cad, he said, was lazy and couldn't be bothered. He would report him in Peč and would also alert Putnik to send a search party if I did not reach my destination within reasonable time. Meanwhile he advised my saviours how many funnel fulls I should need to get me down the mountain. My young men wished me good luck half in Serbo-Croat half in Italian and I resumed my crawling descent, catching glimpses of the bus below, negotiating incredible zigzags. Like AMO it had no chains.

CHAPTER 5

Peč-Skopje-Thessaloniki

We reached the foot of the mountain and stepped on to dry ground immediately, as though a curtain had been drawn to let us out of the raging blizzard.

A string of horse-drawn carts waited on the dry side of the road, their peasant drivers in tattered Montenegrin costume, caps with fur mufflers over the ears. They stood by their horses, holding the bridles, looking intently, beyond me, up the slope, waiting for the blizzard to abate. It was a scene out of the Bible. They must have waited thus for the descent of a Prophet. Moses, with the Tablets of the Law.

Soon after, we drove through the Rugovo Gorge, which anyone will tell you, as they did me ad nauseam, is impossible to negotiate at that time of night, and in such weather conditions, because it is so narrow, wild and steep and all the rest. Unfortunately I saw nothing of this as I drove through for it was a dark night with a kind of haze into which the headlights dissolved; the rock closed in above us, leaving only a slit of sky, though I heard the river Pečska-Bistrica rushing at the bottom of the four thousand foot canyon below. AMO behaved with his usual gallantry.

Peč, with no street lighting apart from the occasional glare from a shop window, appeared rather bare, with streets too wide for the low dilapidated housed. One expected something more impressive for the seat of the Orthodox Patriarchate. I looked for Putnik, just in case a search party was about to be sent for me, and then to where it was indicated that petrol could be found. In the steady drizzle, everything was wet and muddy. A man on a bicycle motioned me forward:

"Dole, dole" - straight on.

Suddenly, from the shadows under some trees, came a shout and a shot, simultaneously. The cyclist pedalled breathlessly after me stammering:

"No... niente... prego" and motioned me wildly to retreat. There was another shot. He hid behind the car urgently calling out something to someone. I tried to reverse without getting stuck in the slush. Returning to the window, the cyclist managed to explain in

halting Italian peppered with Serbo-Croat that having somehow strayed into a military zone, I had been challenged and shot at. He must be a poor shot who missed a big car ablaze with lights!

"Izvolite" - please, to follow him.

Finally we obtained access, through a locked gate at the back of the station yard, to a minute hand-pump where petrol from a barrel rose into a transparent container. When full, it was siphoned through a tube into my tank and again. The man claimed to have given me 25 litres. Perhaps he did. It took a long time. At the end of it I couldn't get rid of the cyclist, who left his bicycle with the petrol-pump chap and tried to get into the car. It was hard to convince him that I was not staying the night but driving on to Dečani, and no wonder considering the weather.

I sped back to Putnik Office, where the man spoke good American. As he offered me all kinds of tourist brochures, peasants flocked in and pressed to look over my shoulder at what he was giving me. The hotel, right next door, was of the barrack category. 700 dinars for the room with two beds, and no basin. Here I definitely had to use my own sheets and towel. The WC. on my floor did not work, perhaps the one on the floor below did. I wondered whether this was the place described by Rebecca West in which there were no seats to the chairs. Ah but next year, said the Putnik man, who waited for me in the lobby, there will be a luxury hotel here. There was no garage, so he was going to keep AMO in his own. Though in a hurry to go to the cinema, he could not resist describing, with relish, the dangers I had faced in the Rugovo Gorge, and at the summit of Čakor, 1840 metres, the highest in Montenegro. Peč, he styled the Rome of the Orthodox Church. It must be worth the luxury hotel obviously.

The Restaurant was run by another catering school. Dinner cost 200 dinars and the students, who spoke French, were most anxious to please.

In the morning, looking out of my window which could have done with a wash, I was confronted not with an equivalent of Bernini's colonnade, in this Rome of the East, but just a wide muddy street lined with ramshackle little houses on one side and a quaint stream running on the other. After a prolonged stay in Turkey, I learned to mistrust the quaintness of such streams which more often than not are open drains.

When I found the Patriarchate, about two kilometres away, it seemed to consist of three churches - chapels. A service was in progress and the sermon went on amidst the din made by newcomers in the outer chapel only a few feet away. Gigantic elongated frescoes covered the walls and ceiling, gaunt, stylised. They were my first Byzantine frescoes of the 12th century, and I was overwhelmed by them.

It was not market day in Peč, and though the rain had stopped the muddy streets and dreary houses were uninviting. The Putnik man tried to get my tyres checked, but the machine did not make it. Payment was refused, and he hinted that instead, a shirt sent from London might be welcome.

A little way out of Peč, the road eventually turned dry and dusty, the surroundings arid and flat, uninteresting. A great deal of traffic, lorries, cattle and horse-drawn carts, raised the dust. Groups of people walking, in picturesque costume. Later, on the road cushioned with thick white dust, we passed a charming group out of the New Testament, a pretty young woman in a long red robe and white veil, like the Holy Virgin, side saddle on a white horse, held a bundle of red and yellow wrapping, her babe; a man in lavishly embroidered costume, was proudly leading the horse by the bridle, while on each side walked three or four women in similar attire. A christening party probably, which will remain in my memory as a living Mediaeval painting.

Soon we turned right towards the Albanian border, quite close, and Dečani. The small Byzantine church was a little gem, with a delightfully carved Romanesque portico, and within, more gaunt elongated frescoes. From the dome, which was under repair, with a scaffolding below it, a circular chiselled iron chandelier hung on long chains. Turkish mosques have since adopted this style.

As we rejoined the main road to Skopje, the lorry driver who had directed me that morning caught up with us, anxious to be of help, even offering a swig from his bottle.

"Falla, falla" - thank you, I called out as I pressed on at a top speed of 20 miles, bumping over pot holes.

From now on the slender flight of a minaret was added to the scenery, until we reached Prizren, an entirely Turkish style town. The Turks were expelled just before the first world war, but Muslim culture and habits remain. The costumes were striking, a mixture of black, brown and mulberry, but there were few about for it was not market day.

The church of Saint Bogorodica, built in the early 14th century had been turned into a mosque by the Turks. However, most of the frescoes stripped of their coating of plaster, were restored, leaving a few unavoidable scars.

I was glad to reach Skopje, capital of Macedonia, and to leave this dusty road. The town's ancient remains must be hunted for. Here was the first city with street traffic since Italy, with many wide bridges over the river Vardar. Some kind of congress was taking place and although hotels were full, the *Portir* of one kindly found me a room by telephone, in a place for technical students. The rooms were modern, spacious and well lit, but without heating and it was bitterly cold. My interpreter, who called himself a 'student in technology' proudly showed me the hot water shower. Only the one marked *'maski'* (men) - was in working order, an indication of their priorities, though even that one, held together with bits of string and gave out but a trickle of water.

I intended to visit the quarter of the Turkish gipsies, puzzled by the rumour that Tito had allowed them an annuity, but no one could explain why. On the way I was button-holed by a Turk who took me to see the ancient caravanserai, whose keeper spoke Greek and showed me a store of interesting Roman finds, even hinting that the quadrangular building of large blocks of stone, might date from Roman times. It held niches for goods and livestock, while other niches above were for the merchants who, for centuries, had stopped here on their way from the East. It had needed to be a kind of stronghold against robbers and highwaymen.

The Turkish gipsies, when I found them, lived in a toy town of tiny trim wooden houses painted bright blue, yellow and pink. Their happy expressions matched the cocktail of vivid colours in their clothing. Surrounded by a multitude of children, none of them appeared to be engaged in any kind of work - why bother, if the story of the yearly allowance was true.

I went back to Skopje in 1965, after the devastation wrought by the earthquake of 1963 which caused the death of more than a thousand people. There were no more bridges left on the Vardar, huge chasms still sliced the ground. The new motel in which I stayed perched on the very edge of such a slice, not ideally situated to induce a restful night.

South of Skopje, over the shoulder of a hill, Tito-Veleš appeared poised on both sides of the Vardar joined by an Ottoman bridge; a graceful minaret topping the scene. It was worth a photograph, but I was, by now, anxious to get on. It had all been fascinating, picturesque and interesting, but after ten days of a spartan life my thoughts kept straying on hot baths and substantial food.

Within sight of the Greek border, a cloud of dust dispersed to reveal a young German on a motor bicycle. We exchanged hardship tales of hotels and their lack of comfort. The Mediterranée, he told me, was the best in Salonica (Thessaloniki), but there were others which were cheaper, but with no hot water.

The customs house on the Greek side was luxurious beyond belief, possibly to heighten the contrast with the other side.

On another trip, I had taken to driving throughout the night, snatching a few hours of sleep in the car; in the sixties it was quite safe to stop anywhere and to sleep; often on such trips on Jugoslav roads, in summer, you saw young people lying by the side of a field, just wrapped up in a blanket. When I arrived at the Greek border in the early dawn, the worse for wear, one customs man, not suspecting I could understand the language, called to another.

"Come quick, a woman alone, she is exhausted, she can hardly stand. And you know," he went on, "if she wasn't so tired she wouldn't be bad looking".

On another journey, in winter this time, a crowd of young trainees manned the border, wrapped up in thick overcoats and felt hats. When they found my guitar among the luggage one of them insisted on singing Greek songs to me. As he planned a visit to London, I rashly suggested, speaking in English and for something to say, he might play and sing on the BBC. Whereupon believing I could give him an introduction and that his fortune would be made, the others asked him whether he might really go to London and...

"Would you marry her?"

"Wouldn't I just!" was the reply, "she has a car, hasn't she? Even if she looked like a camel I'd have her."

By the end of the 1960s I had driven to Turkey and back so many times that I was able to anticipate every fountain of drinking water on the way from Zagreb to the Bulgarian border at Niš, a shorter drive than going through Greece.

A night had to be spent at Niš at a Mocamp near the border, for Bulgaria could only be crossed in day time, and you had to stick to the main road, which was what they wanted you to see.

Germans, who usually crowded these Mocamps, were always equipped with the most perfected spacious tents where they could stand upright, with a flap opening out in front to form a kind of veranda under which they sat on folding chairs to eat their meal at a folding table; whereas I bought a ticket affording me a hired tent a few feet high, green, dark and with a smell. I did not attempt to crawl under it but slept in the car, a new Hillman by then, with a bench seat in front, but still an AMO 924!

There was a shower block in bare cement, with hot water and loos a la oriental, a square slab on the floor. When treading my way towards it in the night, I came across two massive wolf hounds with their handler going their rounds of the camp. It had not occurred to me until then that indeed all sorts of crimes might easily be committed in a situation such as this.

The first time I reached the Bulgarian border it was dusk, and while the car was being thoroughly inspected I noticed a young woman, highly made up, sitting upright on a chair with hands flat in her lap, motionless and vacant as a painted doll, waiting for clients. As soon as I was released by the customs, she came to life and turning into a receptionist, took me inside the small hotel a few yards from the customs pad. It was illuminated, as were the few trees in front of it, with coloured bulbs, looking very Christmassy. Masses of nightingales sang in those trees, and it took me some time to realise that a tape provided that idyllic atmosphere together with love for sale for those decadent capitalists from the West going through to Turkey in transit.

No sooner had she received my money and given me a key to a room than she made a dash back to the customs pad where two Turkish motorists, emigrant workers, had arrived. Hopefully, clients for a last fling before reaching the restrictions of their own country.

The road through Bulgaria was wide and sometimes bordered with trees, but a substantial part of it was paved with rough hewn stones that slowed you down. Astonishingly, not withstanding the extreme width of it, the speed limit might be only 10 kilometres per hour!

Provided no over zealous policeman impeded your progress, the entire country, up to the Turkish border, could be crossed within six hours. You were not encouraged to stray, but should you by the most amazing chance come across a village market where you could replenish with fruit, you would be surprised to find by pure coincidence of course, a casual shopper by your side who spoke excellent English and was anxious to help. It was after parting with such a fortuitous encounter, that I was stung by a wasp to the right shoulder. As the pain spread rapidly, I worried that in the event of my arm swelling it might prevent me from driving. How could I ask for an onion to draw out the sting? Fortunately spotting some Turkish peasant women, I asked for: *"Sogan."*

There were still many Turks left then in Bulgaria, after all the Ottoman Turks occupied the country for many centuries. Not only did they provide the onion but added garlic for good measure and insisted in pulling down my dress, exposing the already swelling shoulder and rubbing for all they were worth with both, to the entertainment of passers by!

I had prided myself on crossing Bulgaria in those six hours once too often when others complained that they had to crawl through it, when it happened. It was on a Sunday, when I had to share the highway with a few comrades out and about, and, policemen. In a seemingly deserted area, many miles East of Sofia, a man wearing a long grey military overcoat with red tabs, shot out of a minute glass cubicle and flagged me down. He required me to follow him inside his small shelter no bigger then a telephone box and demanded my passport. We were unable to communicate in any language but it was clear that a fine must be paid, and paid in *Levo,* no other currency would be accepted. The only available bank would be in Sofia, two or three hours drive back, or more, according to the number of his colleagues found on the way, where he expected me to return to get the money.

By the time I had reached Bulgaria, I had already planned which ferry I would need to catch in Turkey to cross the Dardanelles to Asia, and so time was of the essence. I tried all the languages I could think of, in the restricted space of that box and even resorted to the fluttering of eye-lashes, but nothing did. He went on clutching my passport. Until a terrific roar was heard and a sports car appeared coming towards us hell for leather. My policeman was so overcome that he dropped my passport and leapt out of the box to flag him down, whence I made my escape and as soon as I had turned the corner, out of sight, stepped on the accelerator. Round a bend I nearly bumped into a crawling motorcyclist with someone pillion on the back, someone wearing a long military grey overcoat with red tabs. I barely had the time to jam on the brakes before he turned round to look.

Back to my very first trip through Greece, following the young German's indications, I found the Hotel Mediterranée complete with pre-war atmosphere, transported miraculously intact to the year 1957. Red carpets, red plush, elderly gilt lift, and elderly waiters whose traditional courtesy made you feel like a queen. Through many a visit I watched with interest the return to life of the Mediterranée. Finally its renovation completed, it became too expensive and I began to patronise the new Olympic in Odhos Egnatia; it was good, modern and with a shower to every room but it lacked the grandeur, character and service of the other traditional hotel.

Greek tourism was already actively under way, and there were set rules for any establishment wishing to be on the tourist lists: showers rather than bathrooms were stipulated for each room, for the country was chronically short of water. Turkish coffee (now called Greek) was no longer provided for breakfast, but sachets of Nescafé and dried milk, with toast, or failing that, *paximadhakia* sealed in a crisp wrapping.

Strict lines of conduct were also stipulated towards tourists. Anyone discourteous or trying to mislead would be summoned to Athens, struck off the list and made to pay a heavy fine. Foreign tourism was encouraged and firms were given facilities to operate in Athens. On entering Greece you were handed leaflets encouraging you to buy a house or to invest. Later, with the advent of the Colonels, crossing Greece became grim. Once, when as advised I reported to the military H.Q. at Sere on the Bulgarian border, spotting the GB. on the car they went out of their way to belie that the army interfered in the movements of tourists and were all smiles and wishes, not suspecting that I understood the whispered asides for which Greeks are famous.

By the 1980s all these facilities seemed to have disappeared. Should you happen to lose your cheap return flight ticket to London you were not allowed to buy another from the same English firm but had to help promote the Greek airline which was three times as expensive. If you could not afford it, the only way left to you was overland by Greek bus which was a ghastly experience. Perchance you might have been given an address in Athens where to stay privately. Unless the owners of the house were Greek, they were not permitted to let rooms to tourists. A pity, for all in all everyone was the loser.

Odhos Egnatia, a large thoroughfare on which more new hotels, shops and patisseries made their appearance at each of my visits, to Thessaloniki, is the alleged continuation of the Roman Via Egnatia with the triumphal arch built in 297 A.D. to commemorate the victory of Galerius over the Persians. He is shown on the relief, together with Diocletian, whom he succeeded as Emperor of the East. The palace had now disappeared, while the mausoleum, here made of bricks, was turned into a church just as in Split. Its timber roof was the first of its kind to appear in Europe.

The Belgian consul, a Greek merchant, introduced me to the Director of 'Tourisme pour la Grèce du Nord' and to a French woman married to a Greek doctor who took me round to visit the Little Aghia Sophia church which was a perfect miniature of the one in Constantinople. She also told me her marital troubles; it was not easy being married to a Greek, and her sons, at a French university, were forever torn between East and West.

Months later, I learned on my return visit, that she had never received the flowers I sent her before leaving. The florist had pocketed the money and the messenger boy the tip. We were definitely heading East!

CHAPTER 6

Macedonia

Thessaloniki to the Turkish border

Macedonia was until the early 1950s difficult to reach by road. it is a green mountainous region quite different from the arid dryness of Attica. Thessaloniki, its most important town is second only to Athens, but more pleasant to live in and more Westernised in many ways. Its churches, moreover, date back to the beginning of the Byzantine period and have been in constant use and so they are of great interest for the study of frescoes and mosaics.

Within Macedonia are such historic sites as Pharsalus, where Julius Caesar defeated Pompey, who took refuge in Thessaloniki. Farsala, in Greek, South West of Thessaloniki, off the road to Athens, is easily reached by taking the left fork road at Larissa, but the only thing to see there is the plain where the battle took place. Taking the right fork from Larissa, you find Meteora with its stupendous monasteries dating from the 14th century, perched on the top of immense rocks, looking very much like meteorites, hence the name.

On one of my later visits, in the late 1970s, a road had been made and we stayed with two friends at the Motel Xenia at Kalambaka, the nearest village to the monasteries, built against the rock low and unobtrusive. Greek Tourism is generally careful not to spoil the view with new constructions; but on my second drive in the early 1960s, when the ferry from Brindisi via Corfu, had decanted us, the car and I, at Igoumenitza, the dirt road was being dug up in the process of building a new one. It was a cataclysmic sight. Impassable, but the driver of a bulldozer kindly opened a way through the worst part. It took a long time to cover the 230 odd kilometres to Kalambaka, and I was at leisure to feat my eye on the Pindus range that unfurled its magnificent mountains and crags all the way to the right.

East of Thessaloniki and beyond Kavalla we find Philippi where the ill-fated Brutus killed himself by falling on his sword, before the avenging forces of Octavius and Mark-Anthony. In Philippi today the remains of a forum and of a theatre can be seen in addition to the plain where the battle was fought. Thessaloniki, of course brings to mind Saint Paul who preached there, then wrote his two epistles to the

Thessalonians. In the ninth century Saint Cyril was another who set out from here to convert the Slavs of Serbia, and invented the cyrillic alphabet. The Great Alexander of Macedon was born near by and later when Cassander was Governor of the province and married one of Alexander's half sisters Thessaloniki, he named this town after her. Later still, at the time of Byzantium a succession of aspiring emperors or usurpers needed to secure Macedonia before hoping for further gains. And finally another native of Salonica was the Turkish dictator Mustafa Kemal better known as Ataturk... or father of modern Turkey, who trained here at the Military Academy. Salonica was then still under Turkish domination and only returned to Greece in 1912, in time to serve with the offshore islands, as an Allied base for the campaign of Gallipoli.

The waterfront of present day Thessaloniki is bubbling with life. Cafés and restaurants overflow on to the pavement. They are always full. People here do not let set times for meals rule their lives. While we studied a mouth-watering menu with the Belgian Merchant Consul, passing friends of his were spontaneously invited to join us. The dedicated waiters provided a brisk service, dashing between the tables, flinging: *"Amesos!"* at once - to calls from all sides. Lively discussions on every topic went on animatedly. Conversation was intelligent, witty, well informed, more widely cultured than in similar circumstances in Athens. People were sophisticated, but less cunning than there. Even street cats were livelier, they uttered with passion.

On the sapphire sea small craft painted in bright colours were busily going to and from places of historic fame. However, the boat trip to Mount Athos via Tripiti, on the Eastern peninsula of Chalkidhiki, has been cancelled, (1989), but a bus will take you all the way to Uranopolis. There are twenty Mediaeval monasteries on Mount Athos scattered amidst rugged mountainous terrain thickly wooded in parts, of great natural beauty. It is not accessible to the female sex. One woman only has ever set foot upon its shores, disguised as a man, she was Paula Negri, a film star of the twenties.

From Uranopolis, aptly named, it means 'city of heaven', men go by boat to Daphni, then by bus again to Karies. From then on everyone goes on foot, by donkey or mule to whichever monastery he is heading for. There is however a round trip by boat for tourists of both sexes from Uranopolis which gets to within five hundred metres of the shore of Athos and back. From that distance you can plainly make out the wild wooded landscape over which the two thousand odd metres high Athos towers majestically in its white limestone beauty at the tip of the peninsula.

The far end of the promenade in Thessaloniki is adorned with the celebrated White Tower, which is the only remnant of the fortifications put up by the Venetians. In 1423, the son of Emperor Manuel II, unable to contain the Turkish onslaught, invited Venice to intervene. She did succeed, for a time, in staying the advance of Sultan Beyazit, the same who took Kosovo in Serbia, where Czar Lazare was slain. But by 1430 Venice had to retreat before the forces of Murat II (father of the conqueror of Constantinople).

The decline in population under the Turkish occupation was remedied in 1492 by the arrival of twenty thousand Jews banished from Spain. They lived mainly up-town, near the Byzantine land walls that crown the hill, a backcloth to the city, and adopted a distinctive head-dress consisting of a fox's tail round a felt crown. When, at one of the Turkish incursions, they were threatened with extermination unless they turned Muslim, an enlightened Rabbi, encouraged his flock to embrace the Sultan's faith and be spared. Such people are known in Turkey as: *'dönme'* literally turn-coat, but with no pejorative implications. They are easily recognised by their fair skin, blue eyes, civility and enterprise.

Under the fourth Crusade, the town became the capital of the Latin Kingdom of Thessaloniki, famed for countless outstanding people and events. It was several times rebuilt after destruction by fire. Byzantine frescoes and icons were fortunately spared and so was a Roman arch erected by Emperor Galerius who succeeded Diocletian. It stand in the main shopping street which is believed to be a continuation of the Roman Via Egnatia.

The Belgian Merchant Consul was a most learned guide during my four days stay, and so was the Director of North Greece Tourism to whom he introduced me who was on his way to Kavalla and agreed to come for a ride in the car and return by bus.

There seemed to be an amazing number of gypsies in and around Thessaloniki, in picturesque colourful dress, the women wearing long ample skirts with flounces, like Spanish dancers. They moved about in groups of horse drawn carts. On my first visit, I got out of the car to take a picture and spontaneously offered sweets to a flock of children that had promptly surrounded me. They sprang on me like wild beasts, and clawed the bag out of my hands. I subsequently stayed well clear of close contact when coming across gypsy caravans on the road to Kavalla which abounds in historic places, hot springs and honey coloured mountains, the odd bare fig tree in winter, with its bleached bark and dishevelled branches, providing an ideal foreground for a picture.

Just before a bridge over the river Strymon, we stopped at a small café with its wooden tables and chairs by the side of the dusty road, which can offer such simple refreshments as Greek coffee and lemonade. On the other side of the narrow road stands the colossal Lion of Amphipolis, reassembled from fragments excavated in 1936 and erected on a high pedestal of Hellenistic stone salvaged from a bridge. Amphipolis is within one kilometre with the remains of an acropolis.

Soon high mountains thickly wooded rise on both sides of the road with Mount Pangaion on the left, a region of gold mines in ancient times, while to the West of the river Strymon silver could be found on Mount Dysoron. Both these sources of wealth were essential for financing the armies of Alexander the Great and his extensive campaigns.

After a while we drove through interesting villages and small towns such as Podhohorion, Kariani, Elevtheropolis, Melisa. Tobacco is extensively grown in this region. In 1957 the road, some of it asphalted, was narrow and winding but good.

Suddenly from the top of a hill Kavalla appeared one thousand feet below, its sunny harbour was crowded with a multitude of colourful caïques. After Thessaloniki it is the largest city of Macedonia. The road leading to it is, allegedly, the continuation of the Roman Via Egnatia.

From the sea, when coming to dock from Thassos where nowadays there is an oil rig off-shore, the view was delightful. The town rises in an amphitheatre, with stepped terraces of old whitewashed houses. To the right the aqueduct, which is not Roman, surprisingly, but built by the Ottoman Turks to bring water to the citadel, home of Mehmet-Ali, the ruler of Egypt and ancestor of King Farouk, a fact of which present day inhabitants are still very proud.

On each of my successive visits from year to year I found more modern hotels had sprang up with central heating, essential in the cold climate of Northern Greece. As land was gradually reclaimed from the sea, near the harbour, new eating places appeared, where a delicious meal of fresh fish can be had at very low cost. However on this, my first visit, I had the place to myself and it was still unspoilt. The *Platia* was then in full view of the harbour, with a string of little *istiatoria* where we had an excellent lunch of the now elusive moussaka. These days they tell you that it is either just finished or out of season. The fact is that it is not a costly dish and restaurants dare not overcharge for it.

I have a colour photograph to remind me how lovely it was from the seaward side, for now a hideous concrete building by the waterfront obstructs the view. How this was allowed to happen I can't think, for Greeks are usually careful not to spoil their beautiful heritage.

My guide had to leave me here, with a gift of delicious *Loukoumia*, which are fluffier than the Turkish Delight in its country of origin.

Xanthi, 'the blond one', is the next town on the way to the Turkish border. It is the centre of a renowned brand of Turkish tobacco, still cultivated by Turks. Indeed from here to the border some villages are entirely Turkish, with their own schools and mosques. From their minarets the Muezzin calls five times a day, beginning at dawn; whereas Christian churches in Turkey do not dare ring their bells. In Izmir, a single timid stroke announces the morning office, an army officer having complained of being disturbed by the ringing of the bells.

Here Turks dress traditionally wearing the fez and the veil. They do not even bother to learn Greek, but shopkeepers try to acquire the essentials of Turkish to accommodate them. An amazing anomaly compared with the antagonism and distaste that Greeks arouse in Turkey. When I pointed this out to a local tradesman, he explained: "Live and let live, we try a bit of Turkish, they try a bit of Greek, we manage." Which is in striking contrast to the fate of Turks in Bulgaria today, (1989). The Turkish inhabitants go by bus to visit their country of origin but are glad to return, doubtless aware of the advantages which would be denied them over the border.

The narrow road then barely wide enough for two cars to pass, meandered between hills, some five thousand feet high, and eventually reached sea level. Until not so long ago only a strip of dry land crossed the water. It was a road of sorts. On the right is the sea, but on the left of this causeway are the waters of Lake Vistonis. In places there were bits of left-over asphalt, stones and dust. The precariousness of it rendered the crossing a unique experience. I went over it many times and always anticipate the pleasure of driving over the sea and meeting the interesting water birds, pure white with long pink legs, that favour this spot. Fish is plentiful, especially eels exported live to Germany. Now, in the late afternoon, the oblique rays of the setting sun brushed the surface of the water with golden dust, and not a human in sight!

We reached Komotini before dusk; a market town which Dioclesian had named Maximianopolis to honour his co-emperor. Half the population of present-day Komotini is Turkish. They live the way they might have done under Ottoman rule with the added advantages of democracy and speak their own language.

We crossed endless mountains until darkness fell and dirt roads raised clouds of dust into which the headlights dissolved. Visibility became a hazard, for the road twisted, climbed up and down continuously, and we still had 100 kilometres before Alexandropolis. It was slow going. I found driving through dust that danced before the headlights so exhausting that, against the warnings of my driving instructor never to follow a rear light, I did just that. It occasionally came within sight, then disappeared round the next hill, but when I caught up with it again, I was able to relax and let it guide me, until, suddenly I slammed on the brakes at the edge of a drop. The rear light I had followed on and off, was now over on the other side of the precipice.

It was late by the time we reached the outskirts of Alexandropolis, named after King Alexander of Greece in 1919, but founded by Alexander the Great. There were just olive groves on either side of us, white with the dust of the unmade narrow sunken road between mounds of stones. The banks would be closed, and I only had travellers cheques left, and some foreign coins that no one would change.

The first building on the left was a Shell petrol station whose illuminated sign was heart-warming somehow. Perhaps I might try to sell my Shell oil, as I had recently read in a newspaper article someone had done when in a similar situation. A middle-aged man came out enquiringly. He was clean-shaven with piercing clear blue eyes. This time I spoke Greek. Why sell my oil? He nodded thoughtfully when I told him, looking at the car that showed signs of fatigue. A solution must be found, he said, asking me inside the little office. He dialled a number on the telephone:

"Katina *erchese?* - are you coming? - well come then."

She soon arrived. His wife, Kyria Katina, as I always called her since. A tall distinguished woman with short curly dark hair, in a tweed tailor-made. We discussed my problem, earnestly, which they seemed to make their own, and before I quite realised it, I was persuaded to drive AMO inside the single garage and join them in going to the pictures and later to dine at their small single storeyed house which was some way at the back of the petrol station in an unmade road of dust and stones and then to share the room of their 13-year-old daughter for the night.

I went and stayed with them many times. Once on my way to fetch a friend from London arriving at Athens, I left the car in their care and flew to Athens for £5, in a small unpressurised plane held together with string. We sat on canvas deck chairs.

On the return journey, having collected my friend, we waited in vain many hours at the airport in Athens for the take-off, with no explanation but vague evassive excuses; when, suddenly, my friend spotted the little plane:

"Look," she gasped, clutching my arm.

Someone was standing on the nose of the plane, and yes, it looked as though he was trying to tie something up.

"The string has snapped," my friend managed to breathe.

My Greek helped us get some of our fares refunded. A bystander overhearing our conversation, advised us to forget our plan of going by train, it would take days. The bus was a better proposition. It left at 10 p.m. that night and would reach Thessaloniki the next morning at five; there we had to change buses within two hours and finally arrive at Alexandropolis five and a half hours later. The journey was not all that uncomfortable. If only we could have snatched a bit of sleep. But the passengers protested loudly whenever the attendant stopped the radio blaring or dimmed the lights. They sang, clapping hands, throughout the night.

In the late sixties I tried the train journey from Turkey to Alexandropolis. At Uzunköprü, near Edirne - Adrianople - you had to clamber down on to the track, walk over the border and climb into the Greek train. Meanwhile there was a bridge over the river Evros, linking Greece and Turkey, within half an hour's drive from Alexandropolis to Ipsala on the Turkish side, built in 1962, but the Turks, for some reason, would not let their side be opened. We went to see it when it was completed, with the family from Alexandropolis, and spoke to the Greek guards half way along where the barriers closed the entrance to the Turkish part. It was so very frustrating.

In 1957, there were no hotels and only one or two uninspiring restaurants, but by the mid-sixties, a motel had been built in a large garden with its own beach at the back. New restaurants appeared along the main street with patisseries and luxury shops. As is the custom throughout Greece, this street is shut to traffic in the evenings for the 'volta' when young ladies in their cocktail frocks, are paraded up and down the street on the arm of their mamas. Nowadays all streets are asphalted, clean, and everyone has become part of an affluent society. My friends moved to a better house and soon built their own. At each of my visits I witnessed rapid success and flourishing business. I was even urged to remain, take on a teaching job and make my fortune too! Such was the climate of zooming prosperity.

Now no more dust and stones, the highway on the outskirts of the thriving city, which was in 1957 but a mere village, is asphalted but still bordered with its olive groves stretching to quite a way on either side.

That late morning in 1957 I went on my way towards Dhidhimotikon, but that dirt road slowed me down considerably after a few miles. It would be impossible to reach the border at Edirne before dark. I had never before encountered such a profusion of pot holes. We crawled round a bend into Dhidhimotikon. Ahead rose a flat fronted mountain where troglodytes lived in caves; their colourful strings of washing dotted the brown rock like a painter's palette.

The only hotel looked more like a greenhouse, its front consisting of tinted glass. The old man behind the reception desk asked for my passport to be left, and the following morning I started early. After driving painful miles on that dreadful surface, I realised I had left my passport behind. Retracing my journey was out of the question; so I carried on towards the Turkish border, working out elaborate plans to foil the border guards and to go through without the required documents.

CHAPTER 7

Edirne - Istanbul

Within about thirty kilometres we reached Orestias, a one toothed town-cum-village. Extensive road works seemed to be in progress. Were they really building a new road over the existing track? I had heard it rumoured that the track was left in this dreadful state to make a Turkish invasion more difficult. Trust was not exactly flourishing between the two countries. Perhaps for the same reason the Turks refused to open their side of the bridge on the Evros river, further South, between Ipsala and Alexandropolis.

As I crawled through this small locality I came upon a magnificent police station which was out of keeping with its surroundings and on an impulse I went in and told them about my passport. It turned out to be one of my more successful impulses, even though, against the advice of my London friends, I spoke in Greek.

They couldn't have been more helpful, less bureaucratic, in fact amazingly efficient. No sooner had I told my story than the officer in charge was asking on the telephone for the number of the Dhidhimotikon police. In a few brief words, he instructed a policeman to be sent to the hotel at once, collect the passport and entrust it to the driver of the diesel train that was due in Orestias the following morning.

Meanwhile he assigned one of his men to find me a lodging, a procedure that without any identity documents would have been difficult, so close to the Turkish border, and a place to have lunch. I made room for him in the car. He was a big, florid man, in his twenties, with a superb moustache, efficient but very shy.

As the place boasted no hotel, he took me to a rooming house of concrete and red tiles on one floor, belonging to the local doctor who left it in the charge of a gipsy in her fifties. In the entrance hall a wood burning stove radiated welcome warmth; round it, on straight back-breaking chairs, a few locals sat chatting. This lounge, I learned later, was the hub of the village and the only warm spot. The gipsy dispensed generously free cups of Turkish coffee, which is now called Greek. I wondered whether the doctor ever came to have a look at what went on.

The bedroom she offered me was clean if spartan, at the end of a narrow, dark passage off the hall, but I noticed with satisfaction not far from my bedroom door a tiny basin and brass tap on the wall above it.

My policeman waited to take me to a *lokanta* - Turkish word for eating place, used extensively in Greek. After all they had the Turks as overlords for hundreds of years. Many words used in colloquial Greek are Turkish with a Greek ending, especially in the food line. Some kind of meat balls, with rice, for instance are: *Yovarlakia - yovarlak*, in Turkish means round. This is a Greek dish, the same in Turkey is named, unbelievably: Lady's buttocks, but Turks are on the whole one-track minded. And no wonder, with their women still so entirely covered up, except in the cities. Men from the country tend to go mad at the sight of exposed flesh, so tourists beware and cover up.

I wondered how I could show gratitude to an officer of the law, so since it was mid-day I asked him to lunch, which he readily accepted. In the course of it he told me some of his problems, the main one being that policemen outside Athens, are called something that could best be translated as: Prison warder, in Greek: *horofilakas*. This he resented terribly and hoped the law might be amended. At the end of the meal he gave me his address and his photograph.

Later that afternoon, the gipsy kept offering me so many cups of coffee that it was obvious she expected something from me: Could I, would I, take her for a ride in my car while it was still daylight. She would wear her best shawl for all to see. And so, as slowly as AMO would permit, we did the *volta* by car. Although in such bitter cold there were no promenaders, there were enough shoppers and men at cafés to see her plainly sitting in a car with a *xeni* - a foreigner - which lends status.

On our return to the house we found a totally different crowd of people in the hall, and they were drinking not coffee but ouzo. Including two young Athenian engineers in charge of the road works, who lodged there and seemed very urbane and out of place in these surroundings. They lost no time in asking me to dinner, when I learned that indeed there was to be an asphalted road all the way to Alexandropolis.

Back in the house, the younger engineer retired to his room, but the other, in his early thirties, tall, slim, and rather good-looking, lingered on hopefully with intent. He alleged wanting to make sure my room was comfortable and so forth. Bidding him a hasty good-night, I disappeared down my darkened passage, switched on my bedroom light and turned round to shut the door. There he was behind me by the little wash basin outside my door.

"Kalinichta" I said, promptly shutting the door and locking it. Then switching off the light, I glued my eye to the key-hole and thought I saw his shadow moving off down the hall.

Very early in the morning, declining offers of Greek coffee from the gipsy, I crept out, collected my passport and headed for the nearby Turkish border.

The Evros river, which rises in Bulgaria, and is known there as the Maritza, provides a natural frontier between Greece and Turkey, where it is called Meritch. This boundary was drawn at the Treaty of Lausanne in 1923, where Ismet Pasha Inönü of Turkey was famed for exaggerating his deafness to obtain advantageous terms for his country, which was defeated with her ally Germany, at the end of the first world war.

In 1957, the Turkish customs house at Edirne - Adrianople was but a small wooden affair. Within, the atmosphere was thick with cigarette smoke, and dirty coffee cups were scattered about. The gentlemen in charge were unshaven, unwashed, wrapped up in heavy overcoats and woollen comforters, and wore felt hats. They got what heat they could from a small mangal - charcoal brazier, and were reluctant to face the cold outside, even to check my belongings. I had been warned by the wife of the Belgian Consul in Thessaloniki to make sure any jewellery I carried was entered in my passport as I crossed the border, otherwise it might be confiscated at the exit. As no one spoke anything but Turkish, we conducted negotiations with signs. Months later, before leaving Turkey, someone had the presence of mind to translate the entry in my passport. My antique necklace of gold and coral was described as amber beads. There had been an amber route to the Far East in these parts for centuries.

As you drive towards Edirne from the border, only the tips of multiple minarets show up in the distance above the trees. A friend from Paris, employed in atomic research was astonished by this sight when driving from Greece with her medical student son: 'Que de fusées!" she exclaimed, assuming that Turkey was engaged in a massive production of the bomb.

Hadrianopoli was founded by Hadrian in 125 A.D. In the course of centuries its Roman walls withstood inumerable battles and sieges. The Russians seized the city in 1829 and, at the treaty of Adrianople, forced the Sultan to sign the independence of Greece.

My favourite mosque, one of its minarets curiously twisted as a terracotta stick of sugar candy, dates from the 15th century, as do most of the others.

The direct route to Istanbul was both dull and moderately bad. Every kilometre or so ramshackle lorries stood abandoned on the side propped up on bricks, minus a tyre or two. There was a scarcity of tyres, no imports I learned later. There were bullock carts, goats, donkeys with loads or pulling carts and at night this traffic is deadly as there are no warning lights and often not even head lights on lorries. Somehow they manage to drive in total darkness.

On a later visit I took another road, East of this one, with a permit from the military who escorted me through the 'sensitive' area by jeep - as foretold in London by Lord Kinross. It went through lovely mountainous country thick with olive and pine, often skirting the sea. The part from Gallipoli to Eceabat, where the ferry starts for the crossing of the Dardanelles, is still as it had been left at the time of that campaign of 1915-1916, with scattered blockhouses and road blocks. Incidentally it is interesting to note that those ferries were made at a Glasgow shipyard.

On one of these trips, from East to West, when the passage became open to civilian traffic, I met an extraordinary woman at Canakkale. Out of boredom she waited for the arrival of the ferry across the Dardanelles in the hope of meeting someone she knew. She told me she was involved in the War Graves commission and had just been entertaining the then Duke of Gloucester who was on an inspection of the Gallipoli graves.

I had many a chat with her and even took her across on the ferry to Abydos, on the European side, which had inspired Lord Byron to write 'The Bride of Abydos' and where he swam the Hellespont.

On this first trip, AMO and I soon covered the 240 kilometres from Edirne to Istanbul. The sun was shining though it was cold when, in front of us, suddenly rose the massive walls of Byzantium, built by Theodosius II in the fifth century.

Arriving in front of these walls, you find the impact tremendous. Centuries of history come tumbling before you. The Romans and their

Empire of the East, the numerous sieges by barbarians, the first Crusade and then alas the disastrous Fourth, which hastened the Empire's downfall to the Turks in 1453.

I stopped the car and gazed, unbelieving. Here was I standing where centuries of warriors had camped and fought and tried to capture the most beautiful city in the world, but its walls defeated them; a double row of them and one hundred towers, behind a wide deep moat. These were the land walls. On the other side facing the sea there were others, and Greek Fire was also used to discourage attacks by enemy fleets.

A jeep stopped by my side, and a young American in woollen beret with pompon, came over and asked what I was doing.

"I am looking at this wall."

"Yea, but when you finish looking at it what will you do?"

He then explained that the one-way system inside the town would drive me crazy, one mistake and you had to go all the way back and start again. I told him I was heading for the Belgian Consulate General in Siraselviler Caddesi.

"Ah, that's near Taksim Square. Follow me."

The traffic was worse than in Genoa, but mercifully there were no Vestas or Lambrettas here. The cobbled streets were incredibly narrow and steep, almost vertical. Byzantium, astride two continents, Europe and Asia, was built on seven hills, just like the other Rome. Traffic consisted mainly of taxis, but all were huge American cars having to go into extraordinary contortions to squeeze round narrow corners. Side streets were often built in steps, and no warning to motorists. Others were alleyways with squalid houses, and heaps of refuse inhabited by mangy cats wallowing in it. They were sleek, elongated cats like those brought to Venice from Syria by the Crusaders.

In a traffic jam I looked up to see a Muezzin calling from the little minaret of a tiny mosque. He held his hands against his ears to shut out the roar of the traffic. My very first Muezzin. My attention diverted, I lost my guide, missed a turning, and had to return all the way back and start again. I asked my way from a Jewish couple who spoke French, came aboard and directed me to my destination.

In front of the Consulate, I had to ask a passer-by to let me out of the car by lifting the door, which had sagged with the hardships the car had sustained.

The Consul General and his staff were most helpful. They had heard from London of my imminent arrival but seemed somewhat startled by my appearance in gum-boots and slacks. In 1957 Istanbul was still cosmopolitan and very civilised. Women in the street were beautifully turned out.

They had booked me a room in a fairly new hotel in Stamboul, the old part of the town, as requested, within walking distance of Aghia Sophia and Topkapi Saray. One of the Kavas came to guide me. This kind man was a great help in the course of my stay. A local Greek, he was neatly dressed in a navy-blue uniform with gold buttons. When my father was Consul General in Smyrna years earlier, all the Kavas at consulates were Albanians, clad in their magnificent national costume of red, embroidered with gold thread.

The Consul insisted that after unloading my things at the hotel I must return AMO to the consulate courtyard. It was out of the question to leave him standing in the street in the old town, for the tyres would be removed and windows smashed.

"And we'd have an awful lot of trouble, and paper work" he concluded.

On the way to the hotel my guide had to warn of obstacles before us, such as holes, sharp corners ahead, stacks of stones from crumbling pavements, overturned dust-bins. The street scene at the time of Byzantium's zenith was even worse. Walking the streets was out of the question for persons of quality. Refuse was thrown out of windows, even chamber-pots were emptied thus - but so were they on London Bridge at about the same period.

In the tenth century, the Venetian ambassador Liudprand, was forced to walk abroad by the cussedness of the Emperor Nicephoros Phocas, and he left graphic descriptions of his plight negotiating the sordid lanes of Constantinople.

The hotel had been designed by a local Italian architect, whom I later met. It was so pretty, within and without with embellishments of wrought iron balustrades which he allowed me to photograph for my Aunt in Smyrna, who was renovating some of the family property. It was called the 'Palace of Silk'. Hotels tended to be given such names, even unprepossessing ones such as at Ayvalik where the names Ekonomik Palas were quaintly coupled. Only the few established ones did not stoop to such a ply as the Park Hotel in Istanbul, run by a Greco-Armenian company. The service by local elderly Greek waiters was impeccable, and meals were enlivened by an orchestra. The Prime Minister, Adnan Menderes, had a suite permanently reserved here. He spoke Greek and seemed to have many Greek connections. There was even a Parisian femme de chambre in charge of the top floor, who had worked at the confiserie *La Marcuise de Sévigné* in Paris, where the son of a Turkish general had found and married her, but deserted her soon after bringing her over here.

I had, of course, to go back and forth to the Consulate to retrieve AMO in a Dolmush or shared taxi, which enabled me to see much more of what went on without the cares of driving. It was said that once you mastered the art of driving unscathed in Istanbul, you could do so anywhere in the world. To the eccentric behaviour of taxi drivers was added the twisting, vertical, cobbled lanes with a mass of traffic on your tail, hooting you on regardless of the sheets of ice on the surface. Mostly the width of the streets allowed passage for one car only, hence the unavoidable one way system.

From the top of hills, such as Tepebashi, where the British Consulate was situated the view was magnificent over the Golden Horn on one side and the Bosphorus on the other. Domes, golden minarets spangled in an ever ending galaxy up and down slopes, amidst gardens right to the edge of the water, which was at times turbulent with crested waves, at others silken with the reflected splendour of its shores. To see it at sunset was essential. It seems Byzas, the founder of Byzantium in 658 B.C. was told by the Delphic oracle to build a city by a golden shore. When he looked across the water - it must have been at sunset - there it was. Today the golden glitter is caused by the reflection of the sun upon the window-panes on the Asian shore. What could have been reflected in 658 B.C.?

The British Consulate is based on the outer precincts of extensive buildings and courtyards on the site of the Embassy built by Lord Elgin, of marbles fame. All the Embassies were turned into consulates when Ataturk moved the capital to Ankara. Turks still refer to them here as Sefareti, embassy. The Belgian Embassy/Consulate was an imposing square stone-built house with wide steps leading up to its entrance, enclosed in an iron-railed courtyard where AMO was to live. In 1957 the Belgian Consul General had the living quarters refurbished and redecorated, reasoning that it would be more fitting as well as more economical for the Ambassador to reside in his own

Consulate rather than at an hotel, every time he came to Istanbul from Ankara, on his frequent moves.

I sampled the comfortable beds of the newly done-up house when one night, on arriving from Ankara, I telephoned in despair from my hotel, having found a swarm of cockroaches had taken over my suitcase on the bedroom floor! The very same Palace of Silk less than six months later. Such is the general lack of maintenance in this country, the assumption being that you build something once, then Allah will look after it thereafter.

CHAPTER 8

Aghia Sophia - Pammakaristos

I could not wait to walk up the steep cobbled street from the hotel to Aghia Sophia. As I reached the crest of the hill it suddenly sprang into view, with its Byzantine buttresses in a pattern of light and burnt brick.

When it was turned into a mosque at the fall of Constantinople to the Turks in 1453, four minarets were added to it and stone lean-to all round the lower part of its walls were put up to house multiple Medresses, (Muslim schools of theology), which unhappily gave it the heavy squat look we see today.

All its mosaics were covered with plaster, as the Muslim religion does not allow representation of the human form, but recently it was declared a museum since when cleaning of the plaster and renovation began. But the dome is the thing. You can stand and look at that dome for hours. A marvel defying the laws of gravity. Less than half the height of London's Saint Paul's, built by Wren, or Rome's Saint Peter's designed by Michelangelo, it has a lightness of its own. You wonder how it can hold on, indeed the first dome collapsed twenty odd years after it was put up, helped by an earthquake. But after all it was built more than a thousand years before Saint Peter's.

The Emperor Justinian, who conceived the idea of creating the most stupendous church in Christendom, entrusted the work to two renowned architects Isidore of Miletus and Anthemius of Tralles. It was erected on the site of an earlier church, the very first Christian Basilica, built by Constantine the Great, the converted pagan who gave his name to Constantinople, and it cost in the region of fifteen and a half million pounds at the time.

The amazingly weightless looking dome was made of light Byzantine brick and the entire building was completed within five years; whereas Saint Peter in Rome took 176 years to build with contradictory plans from many a famous sculptor/architect, in the course of the Pontificate of numerous Popes.

As you come through the narthex, the mosaics in the lunette above the central doorway, cleaned of their coat of plaster, show up clear and beautiful on a background of gold, depicting the Virgin Mary with the Infant Jesus. On one side, the Emperor Constantine offers her the city and on the other Justinian presents the church. Above it there is a sprinkling of spring flowers in mosaics as fresh looking as their subject, while on the side walls delicate stone carvings of acanthus leaves are entwined with the monograms of Justinian and Theodora. Theodora, we learn, made a superb Empress. Indeed actresses usually play the part of authority to perfection. Her father was a bear keeper and she had once been a circus performer, and all sorts of other things besides, according to who is telling the story.

As you walk into the immense church, seventy-seven metres long by just over seventy-one wide, you are not dazzled by its brilliance, as when entering San Marco in Venice, for here the surfaces lack lustre. The columns of green breccia and porphyry, some taken from the great temple of Balbeck in Lebanon, others from that of Diana of Ephesus, one of the wonders of the ancient world, can all do with a scrubbing, as can the rest of the interior.

The work of uncovering the mosaics, removing the plaster and restoration, was carried out under the direction of Professor Underwood of the American Institute of Archaeology.

Before the church's treasure was looted, first by the Crusaders in 1204, then by the conquering Turks in 1453, the walls were aglitter with precious stones, mosaics and costly damask hangings. The windows were so placed that the shaft of light caught the gold of the mosaics and made it sparkle. Every conceivable art was devised to reflect its beauty to the greatest advantage. Some of the treasure from Byzantium can be seen in Venice, where it was sent, on the Venetian ships which carried the Western barbarians to ransack the most beautiful city in the world. For instance the Horses of Nero were taken from the Hippodrome and placed above the entrance to San Marco, where they remain.

You cannot take in too much on the first visit, and so, with the help of Matteo the Greek *Kavas* at the Consulate, I discovered one of my Byzantine introductions, which had been given to me in unusual circumstances. I was calling at the Belgian Consulate in Nice, when an elderly man sitting in the waiting room, on hearing my name, sprang to his feet, promptly embraced me as he introduced himself. I could hardly believe it, for throughout my youth I had gazed at his likeness in a family photograph.

"I was at your christening" he informed me. It was he who had introduced my parents to each other.

TEK BAŞINA .... ' all alone she went through Jugoslavia
and no-one touched her. This photograph featured on the front
page of theTurkish newspaper AKŞAM on arrival in Istanbul.

Kavella - The Ottoman aqueduct on the left
and the citidel of Mehmet Ali on the right.

Split - The Palace of Diocletian.

Woman of Macedonia.

Dubrovnik - A woman of proud
bearing in a magnificent costume.

Climbing towards the Lovčen;
the view from the Summit was superb.

A village dance in Montenegro.

Encounters on the way to Prizren.

Ankara - The citadel.

Smyrna - The Agnora of Marcus Aurelius.

Bornova - King Edward VII was received at a ball
at a residence whose walls can be seen on the right.

Ephesus - View from the Acropolis.

Ephesus - Fountain of Hadrian and steps
leading to the Acropolis.

Now he lived in Nice, a retired Consul General, and we drove to his flat where I met his wife and sister in law. A year later, I brought my aunt, who was back from Smyrna, to meet them again after all those years.

The first introduction he gave me was to a distant cousin of his, a Byzantine woman who was, he told me, a correspondent of the London Times. I met a few others who made that claim, the accredited correspondent however, was an elderly Byzantine Greek who never left his quarters in the Park Hotel. A fleet of informers brought him all the news on a platter. Perhaps those I came across were some of his ramifications.

To find this Byzantine cousin of his in Istanbul, I had to negotiate the most appallingly dirty streets, in the rain, with pools of mud and mounds of stones and rubbish. Shoes soaked, stockings ripped, I reached a dingy apartment house and climbed neglected stairs. There she lived with her Hellene husband, a businessman, and her aged wizened mother. She was big, buxom and a bit loud, but cultured and interesting, and she decided to show me Aghia Sophia in detail. We arranged a visit for the following morning, and later, she also introduced me to Byzantinologists from whom I learned a great deal. Meanwhile she urged me to pay a visit to the Press Office, where they would issue me with a Press card, a most necessary document.

"But... but... I've only written one or two magazine articles."

"Never mind, you are a journalist, you are going to write about Turkey aren't you? Well then that settles it."

The Press Office situated at Harbiye, a wide modern tree lined avenue, in Beyoglu, was miles from the alleyway where my new acquaintance lived. Following her directions I tried to catch a dolmush going that way. Standing on the bare strip of pavement at the corner of a narrow cobbled street I was in imminent danger from the projectiles emerging round a bottle-neck from the hill below, and catapulting past me. People stepped in their path calling their destination to the driver, who either stopped when he could squeeze one more passenger in, or else drove past swerving to miss them by inches. Sometimes he might stoop to give a negative sign by merely raising an eyebrow. Should it happen to be the one on the opposite side from where you stood, you were not the wiser and went on bellowing hopefully.

Eventually I was taken aboard and decanted at Taksim Square. In its centre stood a kind of French Revolution guillotine, which puzzled me. On closer inspection it proved to be an enormous monument in bronze to Ataturk's deeds. You could at least walk looking up around here, but there were still obstacles in your path. Past the Hotel Hilton and the Divan tea room, that was to become my headquarters henceforward, I reached the Radio Evi (radio house) and Press Office, which were Government Departments more like a ministry. A charming young woman received me in a comfortable carpeted office, where she entertained a few foreign correspondents to little convex glasses of tea. They all screamed their disbelief on hearing I had arrived through Jugoslavia via Montenegro alone by car.

"In this weather!" exclaimed a young Scandinavian, "I've done it the other way through Zagreb and Niš, in summer, we were three together, but I would never, never try it in winter, and alone". Apparently no one had done so. It had begun to snow.

"Well you were lucky, very lucky," concluded a German, looking towards the window, "what would have happened do you suppose, if you had been out there now, in this?"

The young woman was most helpful, kindly supplying me with large illustrated books on Turkish mosques and tiles, and also a booklet with exquisite 18th century colour prints by Levni, some of which I have since framed. The accent was on Turkish art. Generally when you spoke of Byzantium, at that time, Turks were not over-enthusiastic. The mosques were the thing, and the tiles, though beautiful in their way they bore no comparison to the mosaics, their blues and greens lacked light and shade, whereas the fine marble mosaics depicted people draped in rich attire, in such perfection that you could imagine the texture of the cloth.

No sooner had I reached my hotel than I was called to the telephone. A young Turk from an evening newspaper asked me to go to where my car was at the Belgian Embassy, and wait for him there. As I knelt on the seat to open the passenger door he took an impromptu picture which helped me as a passport in many a tricky situation in months to come. Under it, the caption was translated to me as saying: 'She went through Jugoslavia alone, and no one touched her', a feat apparently impossible to accomplish in Turkey. But I proved them wrong.

The following morning my Byzantine friend came to fetch me at the hotel. We must first see, she said, the church of St. Mary Pammakaristos, which in Byzantine times had been resplendent in icons, mosaics and jewels. The exterior of the building was still standing, but inside it had been completely transformed. In the 16th century a Vizir appropriated it for Muslim worship and called it the mosque of the conquest, after the fall of Georgia and Azerbadjian to the Turks, and the nuns were forced to move out of its convent to that of Saint John the Baptist in Trullo. Its interior walls were pulled down so that the mirhap (a recess in the centre of the back wall where the altar stands in Christian churches) could face towards Mecca, as is required of Muslim places of worship.

Some mosaics on the original walls, were being uncovered by a young Greek, Simon Petrikas, under the direction of the American Institute of Archaeology. A cupola made to look like the opened out slices of an orange revealed an Apostle standing in each slice. We watched, holding our breath, while Saint John gradually appeared from under the plaster, in soft rose and blue draperies under the expert handling of the archaeologist's tool. A narrow stone stairway led to what had once been the convent, now just enough of it left to house a keeper.

"It was one of the richest churches, built in the 12th century." said my companion, "At the conquest in 1453, it was left to Orthodox worship and the Patriarchate moved here. The remains of Emperors were then brought to this church, including those of Alexius Comnenos and his daughter Anna, whose memoirs you have read."

It was said, she continued, that the conqueror Mehmet II, who had studied Greek as a boy, came to visit the Patriarch to discuss matters of theology. Later, the same Vizir decided to appropriate also the nearby church of St. John in Trullo, built, it was believed, in the seventh century and the smallest church in Byzantium. It is now completely devastated, only the shell of it remains. Mounds of earth and refuse are piled on the muddy ground open to all weathers, which was once aglitter with mosaics. Strings of washing run across it, small wooden shacks huddle in corners where there still is some protection from the elements. A donkey wanders in. Could there be any hope of finding treasure hidden amidst this desolation? Simon Petrikas thinks so.

Near to this once exquisite monument are now alleyways of mud and loosened cobbles. Small hovels of darkened wood, with the first floors overhanging in the Mediaeval manner, and the odd pot of geranium standing on the window still. Narrow funnels stick out from these wooden structures, belching smoke, outlets of charcoal or wood-burning heating stoves within. No wonder whole quarters of Byzantium and Constantinople so often went up in flames.

On our way to the hotel for lunch, we drove in a Dolmush past the aqueduct of Valens, of which 800 metres or so of the original still stand. It was started by Constantine the Great and finished in the reign of Valens in 378 A.D. The aqueduct had been built to supply the Imperial Palaces with water from the hills, stored in immense cisterns, some still here to be seen.

Over lunch I found that Sophia, my new friend, was acquainted with my second introduction, who was one of the remaining grandes dames of Constantinople, the widow of an eminent doctor. She lived alone with her servants, in a large house in a narrow street near the Belgian Consulate. I was invited to have tea there the following afternoon.

Meanwhile Sophia, full of enthusiasm, suggested we walk up the hill to Aghia Sophia. There, she fell into animated conversation half in Greek and half in Turkish with one of the guides whom she had not seen for years. He was so glad to see her that he knew not what to devise to please us. Turks are easily made happy with the smallest show of kindness or interest.

"I'll tell you what" he said on an impulse, as we stood gazing at the dome, "would you like to see it from up there? come along, I'll take you up."

Back stage, we climbed narrow stone stairs, ramps and stairs again, then found ourselves in the gallery running round the interior of the dome, but still a long way from the Christ Pantocrator - Lord of the Universe - who reigned over it in a glory of gold mosaics. From here, we were closer to the huge angels on two of the four pendentives, resting on pillars that held the dome. They were unfortunately damaged, in spite of the careful processes of restoration. The cupola above us was, he told us 101 feet in diameter, and 180 feet from the ground. The very light bricks of which it was constructed were made on the island of Rhodes. Many Emperors made sundry additions to this superb building, throughout the centuries.

Being up here, under the cupola, you had a direct view above the first floor gallery and the Gyneakaion - women's section where the Empress and her ladies attended Mass. There were rest rooms, bathrooms and loos for their use. A chiselled white marble screen like fine lace, stood between them and the Emperor with his courtiers. However our guide had more surprises for us. He took us outside through an opening and suddenly we found ourselves atop Aghia Sophia, at the very base of the dome, with an extraordinary view over the town. We walked carefully round to see it from all sides.

I was received by Madame Sgourdheo the following afternoon, ushered into her drawing room by a uniformed parlour-maid in black with white frilly apron and head piece. Madame Sgourdheo was like a china figurine, with a transparent pink and white complexion pure white hair and bright blue eyes. She was small and elegant, dressed in crisp black silk with a cluster of diamonds at her throat. Her drawing-room was furnished with old family items, but some of the curtains, hanging and nick-knacks had been purchased by her husband when the contents of the Sultan's seraglio were sold by auction in 1924 by order of Ataturk. The last Ottoman Sultan Mehmet VI, had been taken to Malta on a British warship. Abdul-Medjit was then named Caliph in his place but by 1924 he too was escorted to the frontier with any members of the Imperial family still remaining on Turkish soil.

Madame Sgourdheo's curtains of old rose pure silk were embroidered with seed pearls. The cups in which tea was served, were of the finest porcelain from ancient China. Some bowls of transparent tortoiseshell studded with rubies. I was to see what remained in the Sultan's seraglio in weeks to come.

Furnishings and objects d'art were not the only things being disposed of, the Sultan's harem was going too, though not to the highest bidder. Hundreds of women, dressed in silks and brocades, young, old, slim or obese, stood dejectedly about to be inspected by peasants who had been summoned from their villages in the depths of Anatolia, through newspaper or town crier to come and collect their relatives. You might think that the unfortunate girls, who had been torn from their families at a tender age and forced to live in a gilded cage, would relish the idea. Not a bit of it. They were distraught. Having been polished in every way to please a Sultan, they regarded with apprehension these rough uncouth peasants who claimed them as their kin. There was many a scene, not of rejoicing but of despair.

Among the few others invited to tea that afternoon, was Vera, a young Greek woman from Paris. We discovered we had been to the same art school there, though at different times. She too was keen to see as much as she could of Byzantine treasure, and so we agreed to meet the next morning at eleven, in the tea room of the Hotel Divan. I first collected AMO from the Consulate, but had to return him to his quarters before the rush hour in the afternoon, to avoid the furious traffic building up behind me, hooting, as I hesitated which way to turn.

The policemen on duty were well turned out, and so dignified that we named one the grand duke. Each stood on a three foot drum behind a waist high rail. My small foreign registered car, bearing flags and place names including London-Istanbul was itself conspicuous, but what was most extraordinary, it was driven by a woman! They waved, and so I waved back and smiled. It took me a very long time to realise that they had not been waving to me, but directing the traffic. By then however, all the policemen in Istanbul had become my friends and they always gave me preferential treatment. When I reappeared, after a few days absence, they did really wave and raised questioning eye-brows: 'where have you been?'

CHAPTER 9

Byzantium and Constantinople

Saint Saviour in Chora and other Treasures

In 1957, the tea room of the Hotel Divan was a heaven where coffee could be had. I had not realized the extent of shortages of foodstuffs and the lack of imported manufactured goods. This situation has only changed since the late 1980s when any goods can now amazingly be found in up to date supermarkets and at prices lower than in the West.

The Divan also made their own chocolate, sold in their confiserie. There was no other chocolate anywhere, at the time.

It sounds absurd that there was no coffee in Turkey. Coffee, which had always been essential to the Turkish way of life, came from Yemen, the source of nearly all the world's coffee up to the eighteenth century. When Turkey lost that region in the First World War with the rest of her empire as a result of her defeat with her ally Germany, coffee was imported from Brazil. Since the country's economy was in dire straits, with no foreign currency, none came; cocoa, and many other goods were also lacking. Now they drank stewed tea, grown locally at Rize on the Blacksea coast, served neat in little convex glasses. In the packet it smelled something like cod liver oil. The only cheese available was the local Kashkaval, found throughout the Balkans and Middle-East countries under slightly modified appellations - in Jugoslavia Kačkavalia - and white cheese Kaymak, which in Turkish also means milk curds.

The milk served at the Divan was reconstituted dried, probably obtained on the black-market. Fresh milk unpasteurised, was not palatable to a Westerner, often it might be goat's, heavy, thick and boiled. Vera told me all these things, for she was staying with her sister, the wife of the Greek Consul General. They had been here for nearly a year and were acquainted with shortages. She also provided other information not immediately apparent to anyone staying at an hotel.

The tea room of the Divan was a most agreeable place to meet and, over a cup of milky coffee to discuss our next excursion into the Byzantine world. We carried maps and guide books and were soon engrossed in their study. We realized how incongruous our appearance must be, in tweeds and boots amidst the refined elegance of sophisticated local debutantes, hatted and gloved, who could have hailed from Paris or London. There did not appear to be a recognisable Turkish type among them. They were the product of conquered races whose women were taken to fill harems. As for the Sultans, only two or three Sultanas Valide (mother of a Sultan and favourite wife) had been Turkish, they were mostly Circassians, Georgians, Greeks and others.

It took many visits and the help of Vera's sister's information, who in turn got it from Turkish ladies, to make us take a closer look. These, were not jeunes filles de bonne famille, although probably they had been once, else where did they acquire the education, the languages and good manners? Now however, they were ladies of easy virtue coming here to find clients. In Istanbul you just cannot tell the difference, a known fact that baffles foreigners. A little further down, across the boulevard, through a narrow entrance with iron gateway, you could peep past thick walls, into a spacious courtyard; in its centre on a high pedestal, stands the statue of Père Ratisbone, the founder of Notre Dame de Sion, the world-renowned convent boarding school to which the upper crust of society sends its daughters to be educated. Perhaps all these beautifully polished young ladies had been raised in its exalted precincts.

Through her sister, Vera had obtained from the Aghia Sophia Museum, permits to visit the church of Saint Saviour in Chora. My own Press card would be useful in future. She was also given a detailed plan how best to reach our destination and what else to see in the vicinity. Getting to a given place was so complicated that you tried to visit all there was in the same district and even went without lunch if need be.

We crossed the Golden Horn over Ataturk Bridge through traffic so dense, and such erratic driving, that a sixth sense was needed, for no one would stoop to using signals. In the driving mirror the car behind appeared to be trying to squeeze between us and the parapet, but suddenly the one in front stopped. There was indeed something that commanded the respect of taxi drivers, mingled with awe, a hamal - a man carrying loads; and the one in our way now was bent double under a grand piano! It seems that anything can be carried by a hamal on his back padded with a special contraption which he wears as a jacket, cookers, refrigerators, wardrobes. This one walked slowly, careful before lifting one foot off the ground. In admiration at such a show of strength, drivers stopped and waited patiently. I recalled the adage strong as a Turk. It was found easier to grab your bumper and lift the car while the other chap changed the wheel, rather than use a jack. *'Ishte'* (here you are) they would say, 'no need for fuss and tools.'

We lost our way amidst hovels, mud and cobbles as described before. In the snow that began to fall again a tiny girl of no more than three, dressed in cotton rags, her naked feet in wooden clogs held by a leather strap over the toes, carried an earthen pitcher from the public fountain. Women appeared at windows and doorways, hair in long plaits held by a kerchief, wearing floral cotton shalwars with cotton skirts gathered over like panniers. So poor they could not afford warmer clothing and yet they were adorned with gold earrings and strings of gold bangles. We learned later that all they own is invested in gold worn on their person, otherwise it must be handed over to the husband. Unknown to many, this situation happens today in Britain amongst ethnic minorities. Later we came across a road-sweeper who kept his fortune in two rows of gold teeth, being his most secure safe-deposit.

Through an open door of old wood bleached to a silver grey with age, we glimpsed a bare fig tree in the centre of a yard, its bark and dishevelled branches of the same silver hue as the door. Two lovely marble Corinthian capitals, mellowed to a pale honey by centuries, now stuck at an incongruous angle by the entrance, suffered the indignity of being splashed with mud by passing traffic, mainly of horse drawn carts. As we gazed at them in astonishment, we had to swerve the car to avoid a marble amphora embedded in the soil. Then round the next corner, facing us, a white marble Byzantine fountain, with carved roses, languished amidst the stones of a crumbling wall. You kept wanting to save these treasures, clean them and set them up in more fitting surroundings.

In the end we found the church, square with a cupola resting on arches, and were received by the archaeologist Constantin Tsaousi, who was working on the restoration of mosaics and frescoes under the guidance of the Byzantine Institute of Boston. The church and its monastery were believed to have been first built in the early fifth century and repaired by Justinian. Partially destroyed time and again it was eventually restored notably my Mary Ducas, the grand mother of Anna Comnena, who wrote the well known memoirs of her father Alexius Comnenos, in the eleventh century. The Fourth Crusaders pillaged it, and it was Theodore Metochites, Grand Logothete (minister = literally 'word bearer' in Greek) of the Treasury of Andronicus II Paleologos, in the 14th century, who endowed it with its present beauty. This learned man, a great lover of the arts, spared no expense on frescoes and mosaics, and the lovely marble revetment veined grey, red and green of the walls. There is an inscription in Greek that purports to explain the name 'in chora' which some translate to mean built outside the walls, in the fields.

When you enter the church you are truly dazzled by the brilliance of the colours, a few years later when visiting Ravenna, I likened these mosaics to the ones seen there.

This church was not turned into a mosque until the 16th century, but its superb mosaics and frescoes were spared by the Grand Vizir of the time, a eunuch, who might once have been a Christian, as such people often were. Later, the Sultan realising from foreign experts what treasure was hidden there, gave orders for its preservation.

The tomb of the Paleologi, one of the ruling families of Byzantium, was being restored in the exonarthex; they were represented clad in gorgeous robes of varying designs and colours on a background of gold. The marble mosaics were so fine that the materials looked almost palpable.

Above the entrance Theodore Metochites on his knees presented the church to Christ on His Throne. As you enter further the entire story of the Holy Family unfolds in mosaics within a series of small bays.

In 1453 while the Turks were pounding at the city walls, near by, the crowds, bearing the miraculous icon of the Holy Virgin, gathered here to pray for deliverance. When the invaders finally breached the wall, or were let inside by a Genoese traitor, everyone within the church was put to the sword.

Coming out of this church we drove along the Land Walls towards the Palace of Constantine Porphyrogenitus, (born in the purple). Vera remarked:

"Which Constantine? Didn't that chap yesterday tell us this was the palace of Constantine VI?"

It couldn't be we decided, for the hapless Constantine VI was born to Empress Irene in the 8th century, 300 years before this Imperial Residence was built. He saw the light of day in the purple room at the Palace of the Boukoleon situated at the other end of the town. It was the custom for Empresses to give birth to the heir in a chamber with floor and walls of patterned porphyry.

Considering the one thousand years of Byzantine rule those who came into the world in these sumptuous surroundings were few. More often than not the throne was seized by usurpers from all walks of life; rough soldiers as Nicephoros Phocas or the son of a shepherd like Justinian. Others often supplanted their own kin and had the legitimate heir blinded and removed to one of the off shore islands in the sea of Marmara that became known as Prinkipo (island of Princes). Irene was one of them, an unaccountably cruel mother who, having deposed the Emperor her son, had him blinded in a particularly brutal manner that caused his death. Soon after however, she was forced to make way for another and fled to the island of Mytilene, where, having no prospect of a return to power, she built churches to expiate her crimes. Some of them are still standing.

Nothing is left of that Palace of the Boukoleon and its fabulous porphyry room, over which the Blue Mosque now stands, but an area of mosaic floor of animal scenes perfect in their cruel realism. Tiger savaging a gazelle, the blood streaming vivid red from its flanks, while another gazelle grazes unaware of the snake beginning to encircle its body.

The palace, towards which we were now driving was only a shell. All traces of roof had gone. It was used, among other indignities, as a glass factory after the sack of Constantinople by the Turks in 1453. It had been a later addition to the Palace of Blakernea where Alexius Comnenos received the leaders of the First Crusade in 1096. Though all the other Imperial Residences had been completely obliterated, this one retained its outer walls and perfectly proportioned arched windows inlaid with motifs of white and yellow marble. It could just give an idea of the splendour of Byzantium.

The Byzantines lived in great luxury and refinement. They covered their floors with patterned marble, beautiful mosaics and costly carpets from the Orient, while the rest of us in the West, used rushes over rough stones. We ate on trenchers with our fingers, flinging the bones to dogs lying in the rushes, while they dines in style off gold or silver plate and 'carried the food up to their mouth with a two pronged fork'. They also had baths, and heating amenities, that, as Sir Winston Churchill put it, had left these shores with the Romans.

In the Palace of the Hippodrome, the most sumptuous of them all, many devices were displayed to dazzle the foreign envoys. Liudprand, the Venetian Ambassador in the 10th century, at the time of Emperor Nicephoros Phocas, left us detailed accounts of living conditions in Constantinople. When he entered the throne room, as the historian Wilhelm Ensling writes: '...finally a curtain was drawn back and he gazed on the Emperor clad in his robes of state and seated on his throne. On each side of the throne roared golden lions, mechanical birds sang on a gilded pomegranate tree, and while the visitor prostrated himself, the throne was raised aloft so as to make it unapproachable. Like the image of a saint, the Emperor, motionless did not speak to the astonished stranger; the Logothete spoke in his name'.

On the whole Byzantine Emperors did not exactly endear themselves to other Christian potentates. It seems they tried their utmost to make Latins detest them. When they realised their mistake and were in urgent need of reinforcements to repulse the infidel Turks, it was too late. In their hour of need no one from the Christian West lifted a finger to come to their aid. The West, in turn, in the course of centuries of strife to come, against this new implacable foe, could in its turn, too late, reflect that it had made a major error of policy.

There were quite a few Christian enthusiasts among the followers of the intrepid young Sultan; among them a Hungarian engineer named Urban, whose canon made the decisive breach in the wall and hastened the fall of Constantinople in 1453; but when he entered the city amidst a mass of smouldering ruins, instead of the beauty and richness he had coveted for years, Sultan Mehmet II wept. To spur them on to the final assault, he had, misguidedly, promised his men three days of looting which he now bitterly regretted. Amidst the multitude of Imperial Residences there was not one left standing where he could spend the night. He had to take up his quarters in a Franciscan monastery before returning to Adrianople (Edirne) until a palace was built fit to receive him. He was twenty one.

Thus a way of life of great refinement, unknown to the West, was lost to posterity, equalled perhaps only by that of Southern France, which was completely wiped out in the wars against the Albigensian heresy in the 13th century. Many artists and men of learning escaped to Italy where they hastened the development of the Renaissance.

There are no descendants of the Byzantines in present day Istanbul, for at the conquest the people were dispersed to different parts of the Ottoman Empire and others brought to take their place. However, in mainland Greece, there are plenty of Paleologi, Comneni, Angeli and other names reminiscent of the Imperial families of yore. Indeed there is one living in the Isle of Wight who claims to be a direct descendant.

As we had planned to see all we could while in the vicinity, we turned right along the Golden Horn, towards the *Phanar* and Saint Mary of the Mongols in Greek *Mouchliotissa*, where Vera had an introduction to the priest. *Phanari* or *Pharos* in Greek means lighthouse. This quarter is now the enclave of the Greek Orthodox Patriarch, who lives there in total isolation from the main body of the faithful in mainland Greece and the islands.

St. Mary of the Mongols was founded towards the end of the 13th century by a natural daughter of Michael Paleologos, another Mary Ducas. She was betrothed to the King of the Mongols Abaga, who turned Christian. It was one of those marriages to conclude an alliance, for the bridegroom's father Hulagu, had totally defeated the Caliphate of Baghdad, to the great relief of the Emperor. At the death of her husband, Mary Ducas returned to Constantinople and founded this church and convent. The Turks call it: *kanli kilisi* (church of blood) on account of the terrible carnage that took place around it in 1453.

We reached the church at the top of a steep alleyway of mud and cobbles. On entering it strikes you as modern. The marble revetment has disappeared, but the plan is unique in this city in that it is quadrangular with a central dome and four cupolas.

The wife of the priest showed us round what was left, which was not much, for it had been looted as recently as 1955 in reprisal for the events in Cyprus. In the course of a night of horror, it was ransacked by peasants brought in lorry loads from their villages for the purpose of creating havoc among the Greek population. The police looked on but also helped themselves to the treasure within. A gold chalice studded with precious stones, the gift of the Queen of the Mongols, was seen sticking out of a policeman's pocket.

The priest and his wife hid below ground, in one of the shallow wells in the courtyard, covered with an iron grill. They flattened themselves against the wall praying for escape, while the hordes threw flaming rags down the grating in search of more treasure.

You need a few weeks of unrelenting sightseeing to take in the Byzantine remains, or rather some of them; then again as much for the Ottoman period - mosques, palaces, hamams (baths) aqueducts, cisterns.

On the day we had decided to visit this side of the town, Vera came to lunch and then we walked up the hill from the hotel towards Aghia Sophia, stopping to take a picture of the Hippodrome. It was built by Septimus Severus as early as 203 A.D., a copy of the Circus Maximus of Rome. It measured 117 by 400 metres and could seat one hundred thousand. Succeeding Emperors embellished it, bringing from other parts of the Empire statues of marble, gold or bronze. Among them the horses of Nero from Rome, cast in an alloy of copper, silver and gold. Also marble columns, the most famous the serpentine column dating from 947 B.C. from the temple of Apollo at Delphi, and the two obelisks representing one the sun and the other the moon, that, since pagan times, had to preside over the games. Strangely these remain to this day, retained even throughout the Christian centuries. The horses of Nero were appropriated by the Venetians at the Fourth Crusade, together with other works of art; whereas the Franks, who knew little of art, melted down the statues and stripped the gold from the column of Constantine to mint coins. But no one tells us the fate of the marbles. Occasionally bits of marble are found in the walls of houses, but what of the statues?

The Sacred Palace of the Hippodrome built by Justin II, the nephew and successor of Justinian, was even more magnificent than the others, but nothing of it remains. It had direct access from the Imperial Box the Kathisma (Greek for seat) where the Emperor watched the games with his courtiers.

These games could turn to violence between the two factions, the Greens and the Blues, representing the earth and the sea; the furious crowds once dragged an unpopular Emperor from his box and roasted him on a spit. After that the box was raised higher still and a safe exit provided from the back of it to the Palace.

These games, such an important feature of Roman life, became less frequent as time went on and by the 12th century they were not as popular. It must be remembered that by then most of the population was essentially Greek, the Romans had either integrated or left. However, locals today still refer to themselves as *Romeio* i.e. Roman. The Turks have always called the people of these parts *Rum*.

Though the people were now Greek, the Romanised system still existed, and the army organised and trained to the level of Legions astonished the leaders of the First Crusade, whose ranks were disorderly and haphazardly equipped.

The administration of government too remained on Roman lines and worked automatically throughout the Empire, but both the language and the people were Greek. Literature and the arts adhered closely to the Hellenic model. Meanwhile the West had gradually become barbarian, and illiteracy prevailed, except in the monasteries and later in Italy, where a Cardinal was renowned for his knowledge of law and learning rather than his piety. Entering the church was a career like any other.

In Byzantium many women were learned from the early centuries, then in the 11th century Anna Comnena wrote the memoirs of her father Alexius Comnenos, long before Madame de Lafayette in France and even the Lady Murassaki in Japan.

On my third visit to Aghia Sophia with Vera, we climbed the wide stone ramp up to the first floor gallery where the Imperial family took their seat and I was able to inspect the beautiful white marble screen.

A tall mosaic on the wall represented the Empress Zoe with one of her numerous husbands, Constantine Monomachos. As husbands were dispatched and replaced rather rapidly, the artist in despair, ended by changing only the mosaics of the head, leaving the same body for each replacement.

On the stone floor a slab of marble is inscribed with the name of Enrico Dandolo, the blind Venetian Doge who led the Fourth Crusade, at the age of nearly ninety! One cannot help but be reminded of the blind King of Bohemia at the battle of Crecy, whose motto: 'ich din', and black ostrich feathers were adopted by the Black Prince and have since remained the emblem of the Prince of Wales. Unlike him, who was killed on the very first day, Enrico Dandolo lived to the end of the campaign and beyond. He managed to divert the Crusade to help in freeing Venetian territories notably in Dalmatia, and then to plunder Constantinople instead of proceeding to its sworn purpose of repulsing the Turks from the Holy Places in Palestine. His energy, coupled with a gift for intrigue, sowed discord amongst the Crusaders, which suited his purpose. While they destroyed and plundered, he collected the prize exhibits which he sent to Venice; at the same time managing to obtain more concessions for Venetian trading posts. Many Crusaders left him to fulfil their vows and continued their journey to the East, refusing to assist in attacking another Christian State.

Two hundred and seventy six years later, in 1480, Sultan Mehmet II offered Dandolo's suit of armour to the Venetian artist Gentile Bellini, who had come to paint his portrait.

CHAPTER 10

Istanbul and its wonders

Topkapi Saray

The Belgian Consul General advised me that the Ambassador, who was aware of my case, would be in Istanbul the following week on his way to Brussels, and might make a suggestion about trying to unfreeze my money.

Meanwhile my aunt - Tantou, as I called her from childhood marooned in Smyrna, and not allowed to export funds from her property there, kept me generously supplied with cash and hoped I would join her soon, my problem solved. Being a resident, her assets were not frozen, but she would not stoop to sending money abroad through black-market channels as many did.

Coming out of the Consulate, I set out, with Matteo's directions, to find a hairdresser in what was still known as La Grande Rue de Pera, from Peyre, the Genoese quarter in the 14th century. From the way people spoke of it you expected something like the Champs Elysees in Paris. It was in fact a narrow populous thoroughfare, with tram lines so near the curb that during my stay a ghastly accident occurred; as the tram hurtled round a sharp bend, a woman tripped and fell and was cut in half.

Tall grimy buildings with small shops below ran the entire length of the street. There were still some Embassies adjoining it, antiques and jewellery shops displaying beautiful things to look at if not to buy. The shops, in those days, might still bear Russian, Greek or Armenian names and the work they did was excellent by any standards; but dangling signs sticking out over the pavement choked up the street giving it an air of Chinatown.

As I hesitated by some darkened stairs, a man came along speaking French; he happened to be the hairdresser and I followed him up to a minute salon of pure Victoriana, with red plush and gilt mirrors. After washing my hair with a cake of laundry soap, he took a small saucepan of heated water from a Primus-stove, for rinsing. Spotting wine bottles of water standing in a corner of the floor, I insisted on a second rinse. That was when I first realised the lack of water in Istanbul. And yet in hotels there was no shortage.

My second hairdresser, also above a shop, was a larger establishment with attendants. The water here, stored in galvanised pails, was warmed over the wood burning stove that heated the premises. The polyglot clientele spotted me as a foreigner. There is a cautious reserve in the locals which we lack and that gives us away at once.

An elderly woman who started a conversation claimed to be an Israelite, as Jews refer to themselves in the Levant.

"You speak such good French, are you Turkish?" I asked.

"Oh no!" she cried. I was baffled.

"What is your passport?"

"Oh, it is Turkish, but I am not Turkish I am Jewish."

I was beginning to understand that in the Levant such would be the attitude of any of the European minorities. The very same situation is happening in Britain at present, with immigrants of totally different customs and race. The Turks call such people Raya, and although not disparaging, it cannot be said to be recognised as an enhancing status. They are not after all Muslims!

At the third hairdresser's they were all Greek-speaking and devious. Eyeing my shampoo and bleach rinse, the owner called to the assistant across the room:

"See that you take as much as you can! We haven't seen that stuff since before the war."

I never let her out of my sight.

"I can't," she called back, "she is following me everywhere."

I afterward said to Vera:

"We must go and see the aqueduct and the cisterns, did you know there is a water shortage?"

She did:

"And electricity too, they cut the current a few times a day. The grid can't cope, so my brother-in-law says."

By 1990 the building of new dams solved the problem of water shortages and new grids that of power cuts, and all in the teeth of a colossal foreign debt!

At that time the public services were overburdened by an influx of people flocking to the big cities. Until recently water, trams and other main necessities were manned by foreign firms. The Belgian representative had been on the spot, winding up his company's affairs concerning trams and water soon after the war. In 1957 the population in Istanbul had risen, but was not quite one million. By the 1970s it had doubled that figure. Moving about in the town became a nightmare with drab crowds of peasants such as one saw in pictures of the then Soviet Union.

You had to flee to the Asian shore for more space and plenty of water. Even though the water-bus journey to, say, Cengelkoy, a pretty village beyond the new British-built suspension bridge over the Bosphorus, took well over forty minutes. It was an attractive trip if done out of the rush hour, with a continuous scenery of old timber pavillions or Yalis, some swathed in wisteria, in melancholy abandoned gardens reaching down to the water's edge.

The authorities were trying to keep the shores of the Bosphorus as beautiful as they had been by putting a ban on the destruction of old yalis which, more often than not, would be replaced by concrete blocks of flats that nowadays spelt progress to most people here. An exquisite yali at Cengelkoy built by a Sultan's Vizir, whose descendant now lived modestly in a tiny flat, was currently owned by the local greengrocer who stored his fruit and vegetables on the parquet floors and let each storey to lodgers of the same ilk. Meanwhile the structure of carved wood was left to perish, unrepaired. In the once beautiful gardens livestock was now kept.

On the other side of the landing-stage, the present owners had solved their problem by building a higher copy of the old yali and turned it into flats. It was made of concrete to simulate wood, and painted pink. The effect was not at all bad; with the help of a few creepers, as time went on, it might pass for old. Better than a ruin any day. Some set a match to their ruin but the authorities were not hoodwinked, and thereafter charred remains disfigured the beautiful shore.

Unlike the Greeks, whose flair for commerce had kept the harbours of Smyrna and Constantinople teeming with shipping right up to the early 1950s, when the remaining Greeks were expelled, Turks lack enterprise; until they discovered how easily they could increase their income by adding more floors to their houses, or build concrete blocks of flats and live lazily on the rents. The exception were two or three tycoons on the American scale, who had become kings of chemicals and such. In the 1970s the authorities tried to instil entrepreneurial incentive into manufactures with some small success.

By 1978, in the vicinity of the New Mosque (Yeni Djami) on the Galata side, where the many water-buses disgorged ever increasing masses of people, an ugly iron foot-bridge was built spanning a road lethal with crazy traffic but few private cars. The noise around here was dreadful, with hooting, screaming small boys selling black-market American cigarettes, shouting shoe-shine boys, yelling vendors of this and that. Flat bottomed barges skirted the water's edge where fresh fish was fried on a fire of leaping flames and sold between chunks of crisp bread. The aroma was enticing, but we never dared risk it. These people too bellowed to attract passers by. Vendors of Gövrek - sesame coated rings - threaded to a pole, were everywhere, they too screamed. On occasion the Gövrekci's sesame rings rolled off the pole on to the grimy pavement, whence they were retrieved and rethreaded into place. Stationary dolmush called to attract customers. The odoriferous crowds pressed on all sides. You might see a couple of soldiers holding hands, little fingers entwined.

The snag of residing on the Asian side was the journey home late at night. Waiting for the last boat, amidst puddles of water on the cracked concrete floor strewn with orange and other peels, empty-cans and papers was depressing. Sitting on the edge of a sleazy bench you tried to make yourself as inconspicuous as possible among groups of loitering vagrant children, with no roof over their heads. They can be up to anything - absolutely anything, and are regularly rounded up by the police and taken to prison. Just as stray cats and dogs are occasionally collected.

Tourists on organised tours, who stay in the Hilton Hotel, a cube on stilts, set far back in its own garden, cannot imagine the real life of the city. They could be anywhere else in the world, which occasionally might be an advantage.

By the late 1970s the Grande Rue de Pera had reached a low ebb, with many shops now selling cheap sweat-shirts and such like, which spelt progress to present day shoppers. Gone were the Russian, Greek and Armenian luxury shops. The street was now known only by its Turkish name, Istiklal Djadesi, and the cosmopolitan atmosphere was no more. Unless you spoke Turkish you were not understood. All the joie de vivre was gone too, for Turks seldom smile, let alone laugh, not in public anyway. Children are told from an early age that to smile is not seemly, especially for girls.

By 1983 the population of Istanbul had doubled again in 26 years, to nearly three million.

In 1957 I used to make impromptu visits to a dear old man who still ran his own book shop in a partially covered narrow, cobbled alley. He was one of my Byzantinologists, introduced by Sophia and I still have a superb map of old Byzantium which he gave me.

Plugging in my little kettle I made him a cup of Nescafé with dried milk and carried it to him with chocolate biscuits, round the corner under the low arcade. His surprise and pleasure were immense:

"It would have been welcome any time" he told me, "but this way, what a wonderful surprise, it tastes even better".

"It was Hadrian," he enlightened me, "who first brought drinking water to Byzantium."

"Hadrian, here?"

"Of course" he laughed, "he was everywhere, you will see when you go South to Anatolia, Greater Greece you know."

The history of the water supply was long and complicated. It had been taken up by successive emperors after Hadrian, and Ottoman Sultans. It seemed that there had always been periods when water was scarce and more pipes were added to the aqueduct of Valens. Numerous other aqueducts were built and the water was stored in immense cisterns some of which were underground. To name only two the huge Basilica Cistern built by Justinian where you are taken in a rowing boat under lofty arches held by 336 columns eight metres high, and the cistern of A Thousand and One Columns, which now remains dry. In addition each house, palace and monastery had its own cistern, in the basement. There were and are many reservoirs or bends - a name given by the Bulgarians who worked on the first one.

Then there are the springs, with legends attached to them, such as the *Balikli Ayazma,* made up of Turkish *balik,* meaning fish, and *Ayazma,* Greek for holy water. The story goes that on that fatal day in 1453 when Constantinople fell to the Turks, a monk was frying his meal of fish on a fire of twigs on the edge of that pond, when some one called out to him in a panic, that the city had just fallen to the Turks. He dismissed the news as unthinkable well knowing that the land walls were impregnable. How could he guess that the terrible young Sultan had devised and carried out a plan to transport his ships overland from the Bosphorus to the Golden Horn, which divides the city, by sliding them over greased planks! In the eleventh century

Alexius Comnenos had carried his ships overland on chariots when recapturing Nicea from the Turks with the help of the First Crusade. (One needs to look at a map of Istanbul to work out how such an incredible feat was performed). Suddenly the large Turkish fleet appeared in the Golden Horn out of nowhere. But the incredulous monk only had the formidable land walls in mind when he cried: 'impossible, unless these half fried fishes of mine jump out of the pan and into the pond!' They did. That, we are told, explains the darkness of the water to this day. That pond has been known since as the *'Balikli Ayazma'* (the sacred fish pond).

As for the Thermes or public baths of the Byzantine period, they were destroyed when the city fell to the Turks who built theirs on the same pattern. So what we like to call a Turkish bath is really a Roman one. Vera wished to sample its delights whatever its origin. We were directed to those near the Nurosmaniye mosques, which were grandiose. There was a section for women on the near side to the mosque. The Russian receptionist spoke French and led us inside a large expanse of white marble floors, walls and ceiling, with the steam rising everywhere it was like a scene out of a dream. On long slabs of marble naked women relaxed, stretched face down, quite unconcerned by our presence. One had a beautiful back and reminded us of those Odalisks painted by Ingres. A Turkish word: odalik means bedroom furniture, which is what women are considered to be throughout this land, despite the denials of a few enlightened people in the towns. There are only three towns of substance, Istanbul, Ankara and Izmir, (Smyrna) in an area of three hundred thousand square miles, about three times the size of Great Britain.

The heat in the hamam was suffocating and I was forced to rush out, so Vera had to stew on her own the following day, while I visited the mosque, which was large and beautiful, its floors strewn with costly rugs, gifts of the faithful. It was built in the 18th century and its name means The light of Osman, Osman being the head of the Osmanli dynasty, which we call Ottoman. On my way out of the mosque I came upon a Roman sarcophagus from the time of the early Emperors, in porphyry, together with remains of others scattered about the garden. This town is full of unexpected sights. Strolling down a drab street you suddenly come upon priceless objects embedded in the ground and no one takes the slightest notice; there is simply too much of it everywhere.

A little way past the Closed Bazaar on the main thoroughfare are Byzantine ruins excavated with the help of my Byzantinologist. An arch, remains of arched windows and columns, all part of a forum. You come across such things when you are on foot, otherwise you might pass them by.

Kapali Tcharshi, the closed bazaar, also known as the Bedesten of old, which means in Arabic cloth market, whence our word baize, is like a town in itself, with streets, their sweepers and watchmen.

It must need stout courage, Turkish courage, to be a watchman at night in that deserted immensity, an easy prey for potential bandits, with its multitude of rich jewellers, antique shops, priceless rugs from all parts of the Orient and works of art, some of which have gone to fill European museums.

The original Bedesten was built of wood under Mehmet II in 1461, after its destruction by fire it was rebuilt in stone in 1701. But not so long ago a great deal of the most interesting old part was burnt down. You have to watch yourself, for with so much gold and precious stones on display you might be led to purchase things that away from the lights and atmosphere turn out to be less than what they seemed. You are also harassed continuously in all languages by merchants whose ranks swell as they follow you about trying to entice you to their own shops. They fail to realise that this sort of thing has the opposite effect on a Westerner who yearns to escape. Unlike India, here there are few or no beggars.

The Misir Tcharshi (Egyptian Bazaar) a little beyond the Yeni Djami at Eminönü on the Galata side, was essentially for the sale of herbs, grains and medicinal drugs, as well as nuts and dried fruit. These things are still to be found but nowadays the bazaar has lost its character and stocks all sorts of goods including cotton prints and linoleum, as well as general foodstuffs. As you enter it through an archway between thick stone walls, a quaint stone stair way leads up to a unique restaurant: Pandeli's, still functioning in the late 1970s, where, amidst starched linen and excellent service, we ate a delicious grilled tsipura (in French dorade) a largish flat fish found only in the Mediterranean, with a marvellous lemon and parsley sauce. The clientele was mainly European, of diplomats and gourmet businessmen from abroad.

Later, we walked over Galata bridge, which had always intrigued us but could never be seen properly from the car. There were only two bridges over the Golden Horn, this one built around 1913 and the Ataturk bridge built as late as 1936. Before that people crossed by frequent ferries. In some places there are also car ferries to the Asian side over the Bosphorus.

The Galata bridge, one heard, opened centrally to let shipping through. It was such a massive construction, with trolley bus lines overhead and rails below, that we resolved to try and see it operating. Could we stay up until 4 in the morning, which was the time when this extraordinary event took place? We never summoned up enough energy.

Walking over it, we found narrow stairs at each end leading down below, where an amazing fish market displays the most colourful fish imaginable and still alive. Some looked like bright pink flying fish, others were iridescent blue or silver. I had not seen anything like it since South India. But here the display was managed by proper fishmongers, who knew about presenting their fish to advantage, and not as there, by mere villagers.

A dolmush deposited us close to the mosque of Sultan Ahmet, the Blue Mosque, near to Aghia Sophia and more or less a copy of it. But here there is more open space, without an apse and aisles. The four thick pillars, twenty metres in diameter, that support the dome are adorned with lovely blue designs of leaves. There are blue and green tiles decorated with carnations and tulips of more than 300 different motifs made at Kutayia, a centre which is still famed for all kinds of glazed potteries, since the 16th century. Alexander the Great passed through it on his way to Gordium.

The mosque is enhanced with large, intricate circumvolutions of the Arabic script and floral subjects. The tulip is to be seen everywhere on the tiles for it originated in Turkey before being imported and extensively cultivated by the Dutch. Sultan Ahmet is an interesting and important mosque, the Sultans came here to celebrate religious festivals and it was the starting point for the caravans taking the holy pilgrims to Mecca.

Sultan Ahmet, after whom the mosque is named, came to the throne at the age of fourteen; he developed into an intrepid and imaginative young man in the course of his short life, for he was barely twenty eight when he died. So keen was he to see the building of his mosque completed, it is said, that he went to the site daily to lend a hand to his workmen. He lived in the early seventeenth century, at the time of the warring Sultans and sent word from the battle front, to his Grand Vizir, to have the minarets of his mosque made of gold. The experienced Vizir, avoided this extravagance by pretending to misunderstand the message. The Turkish word for gold is Altin, whereas six is Alti, and so the wily Vizir decided to put up six minarets. In Mecca, meanwhile the furious clergy had to add a seventh minaret to the mosque of the Prophet to keep abreast.

There are throughout Istanbul cheaper places than the restaurants already mentioned. In the windows they display yoghurt and sickly cakes, but you can have at very low cost, a dish of chicken broth with rice, or pilaf (rice) with bits of chicken. Inside the grounds of Topkapi Saray a cafeteria, situated in one of the Sultan's kioshks serves more substantial food. You can carry your tray on to the terrace which commands magnificent views over the Bosphorus as it sweeps round Seraglio Point towards the sea of Marmara.

Access to Topkapi Saray is through a massive stone gateway followed by others and many courts. The whole is surrounded by immensely high crenelated walls which made any hope of escape futile for the unfortunate girls brought here forcibly to fill the Sultan's harem, notably the French Aimée Dubucq de Rivery, aged sixteen; a cousin of Josephine de Beauharnais, who was abducted by Turkish pirates on her way back to Martinique. She was sent to Sultan Selim III as a gift, by the Bey of Algiers, and eventually became the power behind the throne. The policy of her son Mahmut II leaned towards the French, even to exchanging the traditional Turkish costume of Kaftan and turban for the French military uniform, and fez. Though some historians are sceptical of the veracity of this tale it is interesting that when Napoleon repudiated Josephine for Marie-Louise, the Sultan's favour was withdrawn.

On reaching the main court we were surprised by the absence of a substantial palace. Pavilions or kioshks (whence we get the word in all languages) were scattered amidst the gardens, each named after the Sultan who built it. They appeared to have translated in this way their custom of living in tents. As will be seen later, the nomadic instinct and habits, still influence to this day the lives of ordinary people.

During the tourist season in summer, there has in recent years, often been a performance of Mozart's Il Seraglio within Topkapi, just before the Sublime Porte, where the stage is set with a background of the real thing. Further to the left is the harem, comprising the Sultan's apartments of a later period, all packed together on a ground floor in a restricted area, with small oppressive rooms.

Ultimately the heir to the throne became a virtual prisoner of his own party for fear of assassination by other factions within the harem. He was guarded by his eunuchs, whose quarters, narrow, damp and dark, were just outside his door. Up to the end of the 1930s one of the last living eunuchs, a tiny wizened man with flute like voice, took tourists round the harem.

The Sultan's apartments followed those of his mother who was the only being in whom he could confide. Their conversations took place in a slightly larger room at the far end, with fountains along the inner wall, which were turned on in order to drown, by the tinkling of the water into an alabaster basin, their talk to eaves droppers. This etiolated young man had no other distraction but the view out to sea from his windows, or closer, to the lower terrace where his odalisks bathed in a pool. When he eventually succeeded to the throne after such a cloistered life, corrupted by the eunuchs, he was not fit to rule over an immense empire which became known as the sick man of Europe.

Most of what is left of the Sultan's treasure, after the auction of 1924, is displayed in low domed buildings which had once been the kitchens. A large collection of Celadon, Ming, and other Chinese porcelains are shown to great advantage on the walls, while magnificent bowls of Famille Rose and such, are enclosed under glass. The jewels are exhibited in adjacent rooms, but what interested and amazed us most were the everyday household utensils such as long handled spoons of tortoiseshell set with diamonds, turquoises, rubies; cups of jade studded with small diamonds, little cups of the loveliest cranberry crystal with diamonds, and minute square containers for sweetmeats made of sheets of emerald held together with fillets of gold.

Another cabinet held the gifts sent to the Sultans by other Eastern rulers. One was of a man seated cross legged, Oriental fashion, about two inches, square, whose baggy trousers were made out of one enormous oblong pearl, the rest of his clothing in emeralds and rubies, and his tiny babouches carved out of two rubies.

Further on, alone on a cushion of black velvet: the dagger, made known to the world at large since the film Topkapi. The hilt is made of a single emerald nearly two inches long. It is superb.

In an adjoining room was the little cradle made of sheets of gold studded with diamonds, emeralds and rubies with an exquisite coverlet of thick old rose silk, embroidered with pearls in a pattern of moss roses. Here the babe Sultan slept and years later would prostrate himself in prayer upon a mat of pale turquoise silk and seed pearls.

Further along, the Bayram throne, of double sheets of gold, stood under glass, it was studded with cabochon emeralds; but the loveliest was that of Shah Ismail of Persia brought back as part of the war booty of Selim I. It was decorated with flowers of enamel, rubies and pearls with leaves of emerald. It is said that twenty five thousand pearls had gone in its making.

In the next building we saw a series of paintings, notably the Gentile Bellini of Mehmet II, in an opulent white turban. Then came the costumes of the court through the ages, some of children, little coats lined with fur, bore a brown stain where the assassin's dagger had struck. However after Sultan Suleyman The Law Giver, whom we call the Magnificent, had decreed his Law of Fratricide, children were strangled with a silken cord. At the accession of a Sultan, all males young and old, connected with the throne, were slain, to prevent troubles of succession. Thus the Osmanli Dynasty continued undisturbed by internecine intritrigue, for six hundred years after the fall of Constantinople.

This drastic precaution was carried further, all pregnant women within the harem, were huddled into boats and dumped in the sea, with a stone tied round their ankles. Not so long ago, divers searching for archaeological remains by Seraglio Point, found their skeletons swaying at the bottom, entwined with algae.

On our way out, through the first court within the Seraglio walls, we entered the church of Saint Irene, whose sober lines and spartan interior were rather soothing after the orgy of gold and gems we had just experienced. Saint Irene was the first church Justinian had found on the spot and rebuilt, before Aghia Sophia; he then enlarged it after its destruction by fire. The Second Oecumenical Council under Theodosius I took place in it. The Turks never turned this church into a mosque but used it as an arsenal, for it was close to the barracks of the Janisseries, a European corruption of the Turkish Yeni-Tcheri which means fresh troops. It was also near the walls which had defended the shore on the sea of Marmara. These walls were uninterrupted for about twelve kilometres, following the indentations of the coast, to Yedikule, the formidable fortress of seven towers rebuilt by Mehmet II upon the Byzantine remains of Eptapyrghion. Within its dungeons many European captains, ambassadors and other notables were left to languish, despite diplomatic immunity. Tragic messages, incised in the stone walls give an idea of the horrors these prisoners endured.

Sultan Osman II was strangled here by his Janisseries who, although supposed to be his bodyguard, had gathered increasing power through the centuries until they became above the law. Their ranks were made up of children taken from Christian parents and trained to serve the Sultan.

Mahmut II, the pro-French son of Josephine de Beauharnais' cousin, whose father had also been murdered by the Janisseries, put an end to their tyranny. One night bales of straw were stood against their barrack walls, and when they were set alight all were roasted alive.

Within the walls of Yedikule many an infant related to the ruling Sultan was strangled with a silken cord and thrown into a well, now covered with a grating.

Byzantine Emperors themselves given to blinding their kin and other atrocities, may even have been surpassed by their Turkish successors.

CHAPTER 11

Turkish Poets

At about that time Sir Stephen Runciman, on a return visit to Istanbul, was to give a lecture sponsored by the British Council. It was very well received, especially since it had a decided slant towards all things Turkish, Muslim and Arabic. He spoke in English while a young woman expertly translated verbatim.

The British Council kindly arranged for me to interview the Mayor of Istanbul the following day, so that he could brief me on the economic situation. Fortunately he spoke French, being an elderly gentleman of the old school. His mastery was a tribute to the renowned Friars College of Saint Benoit, which was responsible for spreading the French language as far away as Dalmatia.

On the basis of the interesting information provided by the kindly Mayor, I wrote an article entitled: 'Turkey's struggle to recovery' intended for an appropriate magazine in London. Years later I found the article at the bottom of a suitcase.

The Mayor told me of the progress achieved during the last five years, since Premier Adnan Menderes came to power: roads under construction, increased exports, exploitation of mines in Anatolia. Petrol was a sore point, for Turkey had but a narrow strip of 60 miles on the Iraqi border which supplied only a minimal amount, whereas it was plentiful on the other side.

Furthermore trains were being electrified, he told me, and Singer sewing machines assembled locally from parts sent from abroad. Manufactured goods were also coming on the market, including cotton materials, the output of which had gone up by four times (cotton is grown extensively in the South, and exported).

"A peasant, now, can give his wife 3 dresses a year instead of one." He stressed the immensity of the country. The Vilayet something like a French *Departement* - of Konya, was the size of Belgium, while Ankara is one and a half times as large as the whole of Switzerland.

The country, which had been mainly agricultural, was now building factories to make machines and chemicals. As the proud Mayor claimed one of the most important dams in Europe was under construction. Finally he told me that up to now eighty per cent of the population had lived mainly on vegetables, unable to afford meat, but the standard of living had already gone up by two hundred per cent since 1950.

In the course of that interview I further learned that Turkey's soil is rich in bauxite (from which aluminium is made), copper and other minerals, including manganese used in the making of glass - hence the blue mountains - which is largely exported to Canada.

On the social front the role of women had been completely transformed since the advent of Ataturk. There were already women judges since the early 1940s, as well as doctors and chemists. The number of lucrative chemist shops rapidly increased even in the smallest localities. Any drug could be bought over the counter, no doubt to encourage ignorant peasants to avail themselves of modern medicines rather than traditional home - made concoctions, whereas vitriol crystals could be bought from any grocer casually wrapped up in a scrap of newspaper. In another context, the ignorant peasant is supposedly further protected against himself, as an army captain told me in excellent English, that conversion from Islam to other faiths is not permitted. Then he hastily corrected himself saying not encouraged, "Our people are too ignorant to know what is good for them."

A few days later the Ambassador arrived. He thought that quite a lot could be achieved on the spot in Ankara, but nothing from here. I decided to take his advice and go there for a few days after his return from Brussels. He would introduce me to the Minister of Finance Hasan Polatkan, and would act as my interpreter, as he pointed out, however eloquent I might be, a lot was always lost in translation. He added that it would be a good idea if I asked to interview the Minister, he would like that. I inquired what the Minister's hobbies might be?

"Art mainly. Turkish art and Turkish poetry, he speaks no other language!"

This Ambassador would have met with the approval of the young Mr. Pitt, for he took the trouble to learn the language of the country where he served, and he interested himself in things Turkish. I heard later that he was also partial to the beauty of local ladies, always useful to a linguist.

I told Vera, who was as thrilled at the prospect of our hunting together for such things as art and poetry, as I was, but I didn't know where to begin. Her sister came to our rescue through her friends, who had already enlightened us on the ladies of easy virtue. They now gave introductions.

Our first contact was to a descendant of Mevlana, the founder of the Mevlevi whirling Dervishes who were named after him; the oldest and most exalted religious sect. Mevlana lived between 1207 and 1272. He hailed from Balkh in Afghanistan, and wandered through Anatolia, which was a Roman Province up to the arrival of the Turks in the 13th century, and was known as Djelaletin Rumi - the Roman. I later saw the Dervishes whirl in tall tarbushes and white flowing robes that open out like the petals of flowers as they spin round; never overcome by dizziness. It is an amazing spectacle. Nowadays they perform in concert halls for the tourists, with a two man band of pipe and drum. It is said that when they are in their own holy surroundings at Konya, on occasion they levitate. The stork is the emblem of the Mevlevi Dervishes.

Mevlana's descendant Professor Uzluk, in his large office at the Faculty of Medicine, was surrounded with Mevlevi memorabilia. He showed us the holy man's zikke - tarbush, swathed with a green turban (the ordinary dervishes have no turban) by the side of it in the same cabinet was his tespik or row of beads. At Konya, (the Roman Iconium) I saw the mammoth tespik of wood beads, each as big as a golf ball, which the assembled Dervishes pass along, sitting cross-legged on the ground in a circle. To each bead they say the name of Allah. Professor Uzluk also showed us many ancient illuminated manuscripts and a translation into English of the poetry written by Mevlana which could be compared to that of Omar Kayyam, had he found a Fitzgerald to make him known to the West. Its subject matter is mainly humanitarian.

I later put to good use the introduction to Professor Uzluk's brother in Konya, who had been a Mevlevi Dervish up to 1924, when Ataturk abolished the order together with all other kinds of religious worship, on the grounds that they impeded progress. Up to then the Sultan's edicts could not be made law unless passed by the Ulema, the religious body. Progressive Sultans were defeated at every attempt. Ataturk sent his lieutenants throughout the immense country preaching progress in the remotest villages. Standing in a village square with chalk and blackboard, he himself tried to teach the Western alphabet which, being so much simpler than the Arabic script, he was convinced would overcome illiteracy.

While Ataturk's most trusted envoy spoke in the small township of Menemen, North of Smyrna, of the emancipation of women, urging them to discard the veil, the Ulema incited the population against him and he was torn to pieces. There is a monument to commemorate this atrocity in the centre of Menemen. The murderers in turn were strung up. That was the end of religion. All mosques were shut from then until the 1950s.

Our next introduction was to the Imam or chief priest at the Suleymanye mosque built between 1550 and 1557 by Sinan, the renowned architect of Ottoman Turkey. It is the most beautiful mosque in Istanbul, with columns of porphyry and pink granite from the Kathisma, the Byzantine Emperor's box at the Hippodrome. Small domes surround the large main one, and there is stained glass, quite different from the kind we know in the West. In a corner, a library dating from the early 18th century is enclosed in a beautiful bronze meshwork.

The learned Imam, yet another product of the teaching Friars of Saint Benoit, told us in French about other poets such as Fuzuli in the early 13th century, and of Suleyman Celebi, whose Türbe (tomb) I was shortly to see in Bursa on a green hill shaded by cypresses. I was unable to get a translation of the poems of Fuzuli, although the Imam had an old illuminated volume in the Arabic script, which he was willing to sell. I wish I had bought it.

In the course of this search we were fortunate to gather a lot of new information, literature for instance, in Ottoman times, consisted mainly of poetry; there was no prose to speak of apart from the Fetvas (edicts) of the Sultans. These were works of art, both in their contents and in the elegant calligraphy of complicated volutes in the Arabic script. The Sultan's signature (the Tuğra) at the bottom of the parchment, itself a work of art, was often copied in gold as brooches.

In the realm of art, we would have delighted in dwelling upon the exquisite 18th century miniatures by Levni, of Persian influence, but the Ambassador had stressed that the Minister was interested in Turkish modern art only. Vera, through her contacts, produced innumerable invitations to private views. There, the organisers and the artist, when present, were puzzled by those two foreign women, so keenly interested that they made notes on the exhibits. It was often hard going, for the artist sometimes splashed paint lavishly in what he imagined was the style of Picasso. I had to describe it, just in case the

Minister mentioned it, though to my ignorant eye it looked more like pea-soup or scrambled eggs.

Then Vera brought a more promising invitation to visit the flat of one Bedri Rahmi whose glass mosaics were being prepared to adorn the Turkish Pavilion at the forthcoming exhibition in Brussels in 1959. His wife, Romanian born, also an artist known under her maiden name: Madame Eren Eyboglu, received us graciously and showed us a sample of his mosaics assembled on her floor. There were to be 220 square metres of them. Drawings and paintings by both of them were scattered around the flat. They had both exhibited in Edinburgh where one of her paintings was sold. Since then Bedri Rahmi has gone a long way, even to painting the portraits of the English Royal Family. It is said that he tends to speak of Leonardo da Vinci, Michelangelo and himself in the same breath.

Eventually the Ambassador was back in Ankara and I prepared to go there for four days. I stayed then months.

Ankara is situated more than 850 metres up, and as you climb you feel the air getting rarer. It lacks iodine, as I discovered by chance when I saw a dog lapping up the contents of a bottle of it spilt on the ground.

The dirt road was not bad compared to the ones we had known, but soon the track was thick with snow. There was one lorry in front and one car behind. The lorry was hugging the mountain on the left leaving barely enough space for us to pass, with an immense drop on the outside. AMO must have thought as I did, what if the driver decides to pull out just as we are overtaking him on the wrong side! When I flicked the indicator the Turkish driver behind made frantic warning signs. I gestured back, what can I do, and went. Turks, who are supposed to be so very courageous, seldom take risks, I found them generally extremely cautious.

In Ankara shrouded in snow, we found yet another modest hotel despite its name The Modern Palas. However it was small and cosy with a strip of garden in front. Most of the foreign personalities were lodged here; members of the British Council, which was across the road; Foreign Correspondents, The Times' David Hotham who has since written a remarkable book on Turkey, and his novelist wife Marianne Becker, one of whose books, much translated, had given its name to a night-club in Tokyo. Jay Walz of the New York Times joined us later; his articles managed to pass the censor and yet people at home could easily read between the lines. His wife Audrey, wrote best selling thrillers since a student under the name of Francis Bonnamy. We often went hunting together for old manuscripts in the bazaar. Other well known visitors to the hotel were Doctor Kücük of Cyprus and Bernard Spencer, the poet, who was with the British Council and gave me a typescript wad of his autographed poems. We would all consult the first served in the dining-room about which foods must be avoided. When the sausages were still crunchy with icicles: 'don't have the sausages'. The Chef seemed to be a forerunner of frozen foods, keeping the fried potatoes in the refrigerator and dishing them out warmed up when needed, somehow it did not seem to work.

I soon made friends with the secretary of the Portuguese ambassador, who came for rides in AMO at week-ends. The gardens round the barrage, a little way out of town, was one outing about which diplomats made huge jokes, being the one and only place where one could escape. In the course of one of these drives we were once stopped by a soldier on duty. Clarisse panicked, which was a foolish thing to do, for it created an atmosphere of distrust and was counter-productive. He motioned towards a cluster of houses where he told us:

"Tchodjuk düshtü" - a child had fallen.

We gathered he wished us to take the child to a hospital he named. Meanwhile a party of people were coming towards us carrying a quilt on which lay a young girl of about 13 or 14 soaked in her blood. They laid her on the back seat and the soldier motioned us to go. She was the victim of a home provided abortion. They thought of the hospital only as a last resort, when things got out of control. In the driving mirror I anxiously watched her eyes getting glazed, but did not dare to speed over a bumpy road.

A day or two later we returned to the hospital, fearing the worst. When told that she was still alive, we bought her food, such as milk which had just began to appear in bottles, supposedly pasteurised, bananas, being the only fruit still available and biscuits. There really was not much one could buy in the shops.

We found her with rosy cheeks, in a two bedded room. She lay on top of the bed still fully dressed in the dirty rags in which we had brought her, and with grime covering the soles of her feet. But amazingly she was alive and well. She spat out the milk and the bananas, luxuries unknown to her. And so did the woman in the other bed although she had seemed to be craving for the gifts we had brought.

After a few days the Ambassador was off again, but he left a letter of introduction to a woman Member of Parliament, who would introduce me to local poets and writers. She was a remarkable person, a Professor of Geology, trained at a French University, and President of the Geological Society. The year before in 1956, she had attended the world's conference on earthquake engineering in the United States, the only woman among 400 members. The Washington Post had called her 'Turkish Delight!' She told me to call her Nur. She was very pretty in a severe sort of way, and extremely well dressed in tailored suits. It was from her I learned that: 'Turkish girls must never smile in public, as it is not seemly', and she did not quite approve of my laughing and joking.

Having lunch with her at the well appointed Ankara Palas, where Parliamentarians took their meals, she introduced me to a charming freckled redhead, small and chubby, who could have been Scottish. She spoke excellent French, English and other languages, was born and brought up in Poland but insisted she was pure Turkish. They all do. So did the Romanian wife of the artist before mentioned. However they betray their foreign origin by their appearance and behaviour. Their energy, culture and intelligence cannot be matched by local Turks. Her husband was head of the Anadolu News Agency, the Turkish equivalent of the Agence Havas.

When she invited me to her flat and handed me *Les Poetes Turcs Contemporains* by the well known writer Nimet, published in Paris, I was enchanted, and asked whether she knew Nimet. Did he live in Ankara? Could I meet him? To my surprise, she wrote a few words in the book and signed 'Nimet'!

At the same time I got an introduction to Mahmut Makal, whose controversial book A village in Anatolia was translated into English and published in London by Valentine Mitchell. It sold four thousand copies in England and thirty thousand in Turkey, but the present regime did not approve of its home truths concerning the squalor prevailing in Turkish villages. It went counter the current propaganda, and Makal had already got into trouble and even been imprisoned. Nur Hanim admonished him to tow the Party Line in his future writings.

When he came to find me at the hotel, I received him in the bar, but discovered that he could speak no English, apart from one sentence 'You are a very beautiful woman'! Yet he had gone to London for the publication of his book and was dressed from top to toe in tweeds, sporting a cap worthy of the Scottish moors. I learned these things with sign language and the name of the village of the book Birekit, some 50 kilometres West of Ankara. He indicated we could drive there in my car the following morning at 9.30.

After breakfast, on an impulse, I left word at the reception for him to meet me across the road at the British Council, before rushing over to tell my news to a charming helpful young Turkish woman working there. To my surprise she screamed her dismay?

"Never! Never! you cannot go with him anywhere!" A hasty look out of the window showed him entering the hotel opposite.

"Quick" she said, "follow me."

She ran across the hall, opened a large cupboard, where a man was busy storing books, pushed me in and closed the door. The Englishman removed his pipe, said: "Hullo" replaced it, and went on with his work.

Jale Hanim soon came back for me. When we were in her office I asked:

"What have you done with him?"

"He is gone, thank heaven, he won't come back I hope. Surely you did not really believe he was going to take you to see the village of the book, did you?"

I had, she said, a lucky escape, he would certainly never have taken me anywhere he was known. I then told her the one sentence he kept repeating.

"I am not surprised" she replied, "he is that sort of man. Any Turk is that sort of man! You girls do not understand do you?"

Sometime later, she joined me with her husband and two small boys, to visit the ex-Dervish at Konya. The drive took us four hours. Her husband a naval officer, was the son of a known Admiral awarded an engraved bronze plate by the Royal Navy in recognition of services rendered towards the end of the second world war. Although Turkey had managed to remain neutral, it leaned, unofficially, towards the Allies. Unlike the First World War (1914-1915) when they lost most of their empire by allying themselves to the losing side, they seemed to know what would be best for them in the end.

Finally the Ambassador had a telephone conversation with Nur Hanim, who came to see me:

"Why didn't you tell me you had troubles with your money being frozen? I could help perhaps. Your Ambassador is going away again and he asked me to take you to see Polatkan. We'll go tomorrow, I spoke to him on the telephone. Tomorrow morning come and fetch me at my flat."

The Minister received us graciously. He lent himself to being interviewed as planned, and then she would acquaint him with the difficulty about my money.

After hearing that he had three children, had been in politics since 1946, and his wife was an engineer, I asked THE question for which I had been preparing all this time:

"What are your hobbies?" I hoped I would remember all the things I had learned, what if I did not?

He pondered for a while before answering and I got more and more worried, then he decided and replied simply:

"The cinema."

CHAPTER 12

Ankara - Izmir

Ankara, the capital of Turkey since 1923, is none other than ancient Ancyra of the Romans where tribes had come all the way from Gaul in 278 B.C. to settle in this region which became known as Galatia, and it was to those Galatians that Saint Paul addressed his epistles.

Now only two columns remain of the temple to Augustus and even less of the baths, but nothing is left from those hardy people who journeyed across Mecedonia and faced incredible hardships up those rugged mountains to lay the foundations of a new country.

The old town huddles round the citadel on the summit of an impregnable rock which nonetheless was stormed and taken by Timur-i-lenk; though when you stand at the top looking down, it seems an impossible feat.

Ataturk turned the rocky plateau surrounding the citadel into his capital enlisting the co-operation of his fellow revolutionaries, under the banner of 'Turkey to the Turks' to throw out all foreign interference. A bronze monument at Ulus Square commemorates the courage of peasant women, who helped to keep him supplied with ammunition taken from the arsenal in Istanbul, and carried in small boats, across the Bosphorus, hidden in baskets amidst their vegetable produce.

Setting a town at an altitude of 850 metres on a deserted steppe demanded the energy and purpose of such a man and of the enthusiasts who lent him a hand. Water had to be carted by bullock and horse for each tree planted along the spacious boulevards. At the time it seemed worth the effort, for from this eagle's nest Ataturk was free to govern the country as he envisaged which would have been unthinkable in cosmopolitan Istanbul. (Much later he owned to having made two mistakes in his life, one, in establishing his capital at Ankara, the other in getting married.)

After the First World War, the British had encouraged the Greeks to return to Smyrna and the littoral. The Greeks, however, did not keep to the coastal regions, as agreed, but pushed deeper into Anatolia and according to one version, took revenge on the population for the

Turkish conquest of 1453. The actual course of events remains controversial.

The British Ambassador, bewildered at the stream of ill-equipped, disorganised masses from Greece who were landing on the coast of Anatolia, with inadequate military cover, sent an urgent protest to London, but his cable was crumpled into a waste-paper basket by someone he had antagonised, no action was taken; so because of a petty quarrel, thousands were left to be mown down by a superior foe.

Mustafa Kemal Ataturk marched into Smyrna in September 1922, his soldiers massacring the Greeks, Armenians and others as they went. He then established himself in Ankara as master of Turkey; 'he threw the Greeks into the sea' as they say over here. Significantly the numerous equestrian statues show him pointing straight ahead.

In Ankara he established the first National Assembly: Büyük Milet Meclisi (Mejlisi) in the part of the town named Ulus. The building in a neo-classic style, with mellow apricot plaster, blue tiles and arched windows was rather pleasing to the eye. MPs took their meals at the Ankara Palas Hotel, conveniently across the road. Since the 1960s, a hideous complex of grey concrete boxes has been built at the other end of the town, to house the Assembly and the ministries. Within however, the Assembly is luxuriously appointed with marble and crystals. Members who wish to escape from this grim complex cross the road to the Boulevard Palas, a lesser hotel, in which I stayed on my last visit there in the 1970s.

Mustafa Kemal Ataturk, this extraordinary man born and educated in Salonica, with steel blue eyes and a will of iron, turned the 'sick man of Europe', as the Ottoman Empire had been known for many years, into a new Turkey on the Western model. He succeeded where progressive Sultans had failed, in eradicating the fanatic hold of the Ulema, the religious body, on an ignorant people. He died in November 1938, revered not only as a Father figure but almost as a god.

To this man the Turks owe everything, and so it seems fitting that a stupendous mausoleum should have been built to his memory, on a hill where a Phrygian acropolis had once stood. Begun in 1944 it comprises an enormous esplanade with monumental stairway, all constructed in yellow travertine limestone on severe classic lines of sober luxury guarded by two Hittite-style lions.

The tomb itself is in one block of black marble weighing forty tons. The golden mosaic ceilings and galleries will one day house a museum. The bronze doors were made in Italy. All this to honour one man, but without him there would be no modern Turkey.

Tourists come to Ankara for the Hittite Museum, which houses a beautifully displayed collection excavated from Hittite and Phrygian sites. It is worth the journey if only to see the solid gold vessels ornamented with bulls heads.

Hattusas, a Hittite site 352 kilometres South of Ankara on a good dirt road, is breathtaking in its grandeur. Professor Hugo Winckler excavated here up to 1939; the remains date from the second and third millenia B.C.

The angora goat, from which the wool is obtained lives in this region. Sir Winston Churchill always referred to the new Turkish capital as Angora, regardless of its present appellation.

In the days that followed my discomfiture with the Minister of Finance, Nur Hanim spared no effort to secure useful contacts. The Minister had apparently given her an assurance that he would look into the matter of my frozen funds. But, as she pointed out, "Over here you don't leave anything to near promises." I really don't know how I would have coped without AMO who carried me from one end of the town to the other many times within one hour. Before the concrete complex was built, government departments were scattered throughout the city. From a ministry in Ulus to the Prime Minister's Eminence Grise's office near my hotel in Kizilay, it was a long way along the Ataturk Boulevard, enhanced with numerous statues of the great man at short intervals. It was in a hole in this most exalted thoroughfare that AMO broke his back axle; to give the new concrete complex its due, nowadays government departments are clustered within reach, even though you have to tread miles of concrete corridors inside them.

However, it took months of hard work and continuous formalities to get anywhere near the Eminence Grise. Meanwhile Christmas was nearly upon us. When calling on the Councillor at the Embassy I learned that Tantou had telephoned and left a message that she was expecting me in Smyrna for Christmas.

The Councillor was not too happy about my proposed article Turkey's Struggle to Recovery. Why write on such a ticklish subject he asked. Nur Hanim, on the other hand, was convinced that I would pass over the controversial issues.

One early morning in December we drove out of Ankara enveloped in black clouds of lignite smoke, belched into the atmosphere by the heating systems, and emerged into pure mountain air. It took up to 1989, at the rate of twelve plus deaths per week by asphyxiation from carbon and sulphur fumes, and a massive loan from Mrs. Thatcher, the British Prime Minister, to persuade the Turks to invest in natural gas from Russia. A Welsh Engineer Leighton James is leading the construction of a mammoth pipeline to bring this commodity over the north-eastern border into Turkey.

Around us the young trees, protected under Ataturk's scheme for reforestation were heavy with snow, the dense woodlands that had once covered the hills and mountains had been stripped bare for fuel through the centuries. Now it was a punishable offence to cut down a tree.

We were in ancient Phrygia. Near Sivrihisar, the aspect was forbidding. On our left high conic-shaped rocks stood black, unfriendly. We quickly sped past, expecting bandits to appear round the corner. South of here was found a Prhygian tomb with inscriptions suggesting it might be that of King Midas - his high Phrygian head-dress conveniently concealed the ass's ears which Apollo's displeasure had earned him.

Darkness fell and we were still plodding in thick snow to complete the 425 kilometres to Bursa, our stop for the night. On the map it seemed an unnecessary detour to reach Smyrna, but this route was more reliable than the direct alternative. Suddenly we appeared to be in the middle of a field of virgin snow. The feeling was that of being lost at sea. No landmark, no sign posting unless of course they had all disappeared under the snow. I got out of the car with a torch; there must be a sign-somewhere! I walked as far as the headlights reached, nothing. A drop. A chasm! I swallowed. Very hard. I reversed carefully getting out often to investigate. At last I saw a house, a hut rather.

"Bursa?"

The old woman who came to the door was joined by an old man who pointed towards the back of the house.

"Yol?" (road) I asked to make sure.

"Evet, yol var" (literally: yes road there is).

We crawled until reassured by ruts made by cart wheels. At the entry to Bursa, notices indicated the way to the Tchelik Palas Oteli - this time the palace was not of silk but of steel. Steel girders probably against earthquakes.

There were few people in the dining-room for the winter sports season was only just beginning. This was a skiing resort on the slopes of Uludag, the Mysian Olympus, altitude 7,634 feet, towering over us. According to legend Europa had been abducted by Zeus in the shape of a bull, not far from here.

However *Brusa* had been a spa from remote antiquity. It is believed to have been founded by Prusas I, King of Bithynia in the 3rd century B.C. It was his successor Prusas II, who gave refuge to the defeated Hannibal who took his own life when suspecting that his host was about to deliver him to the Romans. After the Romans in the Ist century B.C. *Brusa* remained a Byzantine possession until the 14th century A.D.; it was then that the Ottoman Turks, routed from a short occupation by the First Crusade in 1096, returned to stay.

Justinian built a palace here and Theodora's marble bath can still be seen, but the mosques and the Türbes (tombs) of the Sultans are the most interesting features remaining. The Türbes are large domed monuments, though in that of Mural II (father of the conqueror of Constantinople) a square opening has been left at the top in answer to this Sultan's wish 'that Allah's rain should refresh his soul'.

The türbe of the eldest son of Suleyman the Lawgiver, Djem, is here too. He was greatly beloved of the people but the Russian born harem favourite Roxelana, plotted against him to secure the throne for her own son. He managed to escape to Malta, but you will be told locally: 'the Templars of Malta sold him to the Pope, who tried to make a Christian of him'. Eventually, the story goes: 'he was lured to the Court of Francis I of France where, he was poisoned'.

Suleyman was the last truly 'Magnificent' Sultan, after his death in 1566 the Sultanate and the Ottoman Empire went into a steady decline. The degeneration of power beginning at the definitive defeat of the Turks before the walls of Vienna.

The mulberry tree thrives here and with it the silk worm. Bursa silk was renowned all over Turkey until in the 1960s, through a not uncommon oversight, many of the mulberry trees were cut down and consequently silk vanished from the market. Fortunately however, in this climate trees grow quickly, and when the blunder was recognised, towards the end of the 1970s Bursa silk reappeared.

From Bursa to Smyrna is 385 kilometres over a vast arid plateau, and before darkness fell I thought I better fill up with petrol. But my back was not behaving too well and I dared not lift the heavy jerrycan. Sighting a flock of sheep I beckoned to the shepherd a primitive man enturbaned in a striped yellow cloth, with black moustaches and crescent shaped knife thrust through his draped belt, but most obliging. I noticed that his feet were bandaged with rags in place of footwear. Although so poor he was reluctant to accept money, thanking me by bowing low touching his heart, lips and forehead with his right hand. The minimal sum would keep him for a week. It was Christmas Eve, I spared a thought for Good King Wenceslas.

We had left the snow far behind; here the ground was brown with pine needles. We were steadily descending between thick woods and luxuriant hedgerows. I stopped to investigate their interesting vegetation and in the failing light spotted a pale orange prickly fruit the size of a cherry. Kumara! that's what my Greek Nanny, suddenly emerging from the dim past, had called this fruit. I gingerly bit into it. It was juicy and a bit sharp. The stars gradually spread over a dark blue luminous sky as seen in the Eastern Mediterranean. Not so far South of here the Three Kings had followed a star to the stable, and up this mountain amidst these woods it really felt like Christmas Eve as it must have been then.

After reaching the plain we drove towards Akhisar - ancient Thyateira, one of the Seven Churches of the Apocalypse. You tripped over history and mythology everywhere in this land.

Entering Akhisar, the road is so straight it must be a Roman way, I consulted the map by torch light beside the first houses. Izmir, Smyrna, appeared quite close, and the straight road went on, it seemed, but maps may be misleading. When I enquired from a passer-by, he told me in broken French that it was a long way to Izmir, a very long difficult way. Yes I could telephone from the post office, please to follow him. Every time I thanked him he said: *"Qu'a cela ne tienne"* what could he mean?

Eventually I got through to the office of Tantou's insurance man, a Salonica Turk with excellent French.

"Your Aunt is expecting you at the Izmir Palas" he said, "there is some kind of flood in her house, and she has moved to the hotel for Christmas."

Being unable to reach me after I had left Ankara, she had decided to send 'runners' as he put it, to intercept me at the cross-roads on my descent into Bornova. When he heard where I was he exclaimed:

"Dear me! You still have a nasty bit of road ahead, be careful, go very slowly, I shall tell your Aunt to expect you very late".

We reached Manisa, ancient Magnisia of Sypilus. (There is another Magnisia, South of Smyrna, near the river Meander (hence the verb to meander) This Magnisia here saw Alexander the Great, then the Romans, and it was rebuilt under Tiberius, after a terrible earthquake. Later the Byzantine Emperor on the run from the Fourth Crusade, took refuge here. Timur-i-Lenk stormed it, as usual and then went on to sack Smyrna. The Greeks occupied it again after the First World War, before being routed by Ataturk and his army on their way South in 1922.

In the centre of the town, at the foot of Mount Sypilus, a giant rock ever dripping wet, in the shape of a weeping woman is supposed to be Niobe turned to stone at the sight of her sons and daughters pierced to death by the arrows of Apollo and Diana whom she had offended.

We came to a fork in the unmade, narrow, dusty road, without any sign to indicate which way led to Izmir. A large square house stood on the left, the worse for wear, as you see all over these parts, abandoned by the fleeing Greeks in 1922. It looked now like barracks. Standing on a stone I reached up to the bare lighted windows and tapped on the glass to attract attention. A sergeant rushed out, followed by a handful of soldiers at a trot.

"Izmir?" I asked pointing to the twin roads ahead.

He most obligingly sent one of his men to stand by the right road and bade me: *"Güle, güle"* (happy be your way).

The way, far from being a 'happy one' was a real nightmare. We were soon engulfed in a cloud of dust raised by AMO, on a rutted, twisting, dipping mule track. It felt like rolling through talcum powder. The levels were changing so abruptly and unexpectedly, impossible to spot in time through the dust. Occasionally down the drop on the outside could be dimly discerned a jumble of broken up carts, their wheels sticking up as they had fallen.

Finally exhausted, I emerged above Bornova where Ataturk had stopped one morning with his troops and looked down on Smyrna. At night the view was fairy-like, with myriads of twinkling lights covering the distant hills as a mantle of small diamonds. The atmosphere over here, induces the twinkling, and at that time there was no neon lighting to spoil the effect.

At the bottom by the cross-roads we found Tantou's promised 'runners' who sprang to their feet and waved me to stop. Two Cretan brothers, Husein and Hasan, Turks whose mother tongue was Greek, tall and well built like Andartes, but somehow I could not visualise them as runners.

"Yasu!" they greeted me in Greek, *"Kalosorise"* (welcome).

They came on board and told me all about *"Ti Madami."* They spoke the Greek of the islands as most Greek speaking people do in Smyrna. When I told them about the shepherd and the soldiers, they were horrified, and warned never again to trust to such people who raped women, and then cut them to pieces, so that they would not tell. Especially foreign women, who they imagine would not be missed. Though I laughed at them just then, if the newspapers were to be believed, such things were occasionally reported, but as far as I was concerned they were proved wrong 'nobody touched me' not even in Turkey!

CHAPTER 13

Christmas in Smyrna

We drove through the main avenue of Bornova, in those days still bordered with old plane trees. On either side stretched large gardens in front of comfortable colonial style houses, some with colonnaded porticos, where the descendants of the 18th century English merchants lived in Victorian style with many servants. Despite their formal way of life many of them had never been to England and their speech was oddly accented and interlaced with Greek, Italian and other tongues.

Smyrna looked more or less as I remembered it, with marble fronted residences along the water front (Les Quais), and horse drawn carriages (carozzas) which the Turks now call Phaeton, but spell phonetically faeton, convinced that it is a Turkish word.

There was still that whiff of horse dung, and old leather, perhaps more pungent now, but mercifully the roads were asphalted, no longer paved with toe-breaking stone slabs.

On reaching the hotel at the other end of Les Quais, my two Andartes dashed to fetch Tantou, who was waiting visibly relived to see me.

"Well, *enfin!*" she cried, hugging me, "I was so worried, they say you were driving through terrible country."

Her fragility was deceptive, for she was strong willed, and business-like. My recent exploits paled before her own achievements, for she had, in her youth, been an intrepid horsewoman, exploring the wilds of Anatolia. She caught me by the arm and pushed me in the lift. We were dining with English friends of hers.

"Put on something *convenable*," she called when my bags were brought up. She wore one of her Paris creations and though quite a few years old, it still retained that *chic* which seems eternal to their kind.

I told her of my trials in Ankara during the short drive to our friends.

"I wonder" she mused, asking, "are you really making any progress in Ankara? Or are we spending all that money for nothing."

I understood her doubts, after all she knew the country and its people, which I did not. She went on:

"You must not always believe people's promises. Sometimes they just want to get rid of you. Why is the Ambassador not dealing with the matter personally, as he gave me to understand?"

I told her there was a rumour that he was being recalled, adding:

"But the most helpful person at that Embassy, is a Belgian woman, the Ambassador's closest assistant. She is married to a Turk who was high up in a Ministry in the last administration and has useful contacts."

On Christmas day Tantou showed me her rebuilding of my grandfather's house into flats. She was the very first in the town to have thought of converting old property. She told me how, when she undertook her first building early in 1952, the authorities restricted the height to four storeys only, the maximum weight, they alleged, the reclaimed waterfront could bear. They were right. Since then, higher buildings have caused subsidence and in winter floods often force people to exit on pontoons from the first floors of buildings. Cars left stationary on the streets, float aimlessly and collide adrift.

Tantou did not want the house pulled down, but extended, and she tried to save the beautiful painted ceilings. The architect, a young Greek trained in Belgium, pointed out in vain that when the ceilings were lowered to make another floor, the rich frescoes would be overpoweringly close. I was on Tantou's side remembering the lofty painted rooms from childhood. She told me how she had got round the ghastly custom of slaughtering a sheep when laying the foundations by offering her workmen a cockerel, pointing out that they were only adding to what was already there; and a bird was so much cheaper.

Away from the company of our English friends there was no feeling of Christmas, in a Muslim country it was a working day like any other; each of the various religions shutting their shops on different days. Jews were the most numerous of the minorities at the time. Few Orthodox Greeks remained since the mass expulsions in the mid 1950s. Catholics and Anglicans were still tied down by extensive lands and property, now let to local peasants drifting into the town. Most of these peasants were rich in terms of cash, which was never invested, a practice that was considered shameful. Money therefore remained idle, often stuffed under a mattress. It took a very long time for American films and lately television to change this custom which still remains among peasants living in remote parts of the country.

We went to inspect my own houses, which occupied one side of a whole street and shops round the corner. Husein and his brother Hasan, tenants in one of my shops, rushed out to greet us:

"Kalosoriste" (welcome). They could not know that I did not care a fig for any of it. I had inherited that property from my mother, Tantou's sister, who held it from her father. My French grandfather had brought over his fortune in the last century and invested here, in the days when Smyrna was a thriving cosmopolitan city.

Many were the European companies who traded with the Ottoman Sultan. The waterfront *Les Quais*, had been reclaimed from the sea by a French concern who levied a toll on it for many years. Their descendants still lived here, in princely style.

The water company's manholes still bore on them: *Compagnie des Eaux de Smyrne*. The trams were Belgian. The open sided tram (in French *balladeuse*) was pulled by a horse along the water front, in summer it wore a straw hat through which its ears stuck, to protect it from the deadly sun. When my grandfather needed to build his swimming pool, a channel was dug from the house to the water's edge, with a plank over it. The tram fare was paid as far as his house, then passengers walked over the plank and entered the other tram on the other side, and the tram stop was named after him.

The sea then, was clear and pure, green and transparent, full of fish and shoals of dolphins.

Up to September 1922, when the heat of the summer's day was spent, maids carried rattan chairs on to the colourful tiled private pavement outside each house. There the ladies, dressed with care, sat and talked greeted by passers-by. Men doffed hats and stopped to chat, nannies carried babies in the crook of an arm. It was a mixture of the Greek volta, the Avenue du Bois in Paris and Hyde Park in London.

On that fateful night of 1922, Europeans prudently displayed their national flags from balconies. The Greeks and Armenians had already fled, leaving all their possessions behind. Their houses were taken over by the masses who swarmed into the town in the wake of the Turkish army. Many of today's large landowners have no title deeds; they just walked in as the Greeks walked out.

In the palatial marble fronted homes *sur les Quais* when electricity, which had only recently arrived in Smyrna, was re-established and the lights suddenly blazed from crystal chandeliers, the peasants were terrified at the crystal devils glaring down at them. They beat and smashed them with sticks.

Thereafter they lived mainly at the back, keeping all shutters closed on the street side. Although they would keep a state bedroom as they found it, with embroidered linen on the bed, they slept on the floor beside it, rolling up their bedding as they had done for centuries of nomadic life in tents.

After 1922 not a soul was to be seen on the deserted *Quais*, per chance a horse carriage looking hopelessly for a fare, whose clip clop resounded the length of the waterfront like a sad echo of things past, a way of life had gone for ever.

In the 1950s, the more emancipated sometimes threw open their downstairs shutters at night showing in the lighted room a dinner table laid with the silver and crystal they had found. The new owners themselves, however, remained in the kitchen quarters at the back.

By the late 1960s, a new generation influenced by Western films and television persuaded their elders to stroll in the streets in the evenings. Amazed by the noise and unusual animation, Europeans rushed to the windows, the streets were transformed! Just like that, overnight. The people have never looked back. Nowadays, they live in their concrete blocks of flats with all lights on, curtains open for all to see. It is the Europeans who now seek privacy behind drawn curtains. So the world goes round.

CHAPTER 14

Smyrna named after an Amazon

Smyrna - Izmir, with its beautiful bay surrounded by blue mountains sheltering a uniquely situated harbour, was famed throughout antiquity, and remains even now the outlet for the wealth of Anatolia. The wharfs and harbour precincts are forever stacked with cases of figs, raisins, tobacco, cotton, to mention only a few, among them vallonia, which is exported extensively to Great Britain and is the basis for the renowned fast dyes. Up to the 1970s many of these goods were brought from the interior by caravans of camels softly padding along with the single dong of the leader's bell.

Smyrna was named after an Amazon and so was Ephesus, and according to Strabo, they were a nation of warlike women greatly feared in this part of the world, and the stories of their deeds are depicted on pediments and sarcophagi. Once a year they raided a tribe of their choice and took away the men, from these unions they kept the female offspring and returned the males to the tribe who had fathered them. Although in this region mythology is often intermingled with history, some experts believe that the Amazons should belong to the latter.

The Roman Agora that can still be seen in Smyrna today, was rebuilt after an earthquake, by Marcus Aurelius over the remains of the Greek one. Whereas across the bay on the site of present day Karshiyaka, Richard-Coeur-de-Lion camped with his crusaders, on his way to the Holy Land, and the place named after him, was still known as Cordeleo as late as 1922.

Up to the 1970s, before hideous concrete blocks of flats replaced the elegant marble fronted residences on its waterfront, the view across the bay towards Smyrna at night, had to be seen to be believed.

In those days no neon lighting could spoil a scene, whose backcloth of undulating hills sparkled with twinkling lights against the deep blue velvet of the night sky. At the summit of the highest of the Pagus Hills, Alexander the Great rebuilt the town in a more impregnable situation. In his dream, recounted down the centuries, he had seen the two Nemeses goddesses, (known elsewhere as the one Nemesis) who were worshipped in Smyrna; they urged him to rebuild the city which had remained ruined for three centuries. The twin peaks overlooking the bay bore their name, but since the Head-Quarters of N.A.T.O. in the Eastern Mediterranean are in Smyrna - Izmir, American G.I.s have renamed them Marylin Monroe!

The city of Smyrna, at the top of Mount Pagus, held against invasion for over a thousand years, but finally it fell to the same Timur-i-Lenk who had stormed Ancyra. He slew the entire population, and it is said that only one man escaped.

There is quite a lot to see up there, even to the original Hellenistic walls, amidst pines and olive groves, with sumptuous views over the Gulf of Smyrna on one side and on the other, to the North, the village of Bornova nestling at the foot of hills which in spring are a mass of anemones. King Edward VII was once received at a ball, in one of the opulent residences belonging to descendants of English merchants settled here since the 18th century.

Budja, situated Eastwards, was another stronghold of the English of past centuries. In the precincts of its church of flint, which could have been moved straight from an English suburb, lie the remains of: 'Francis Werry, merchant of Smyrna, born in Cornwall, H.B.MAJ. Consul'.

An Avenue of gigantic cypresses leading to his house, where Lord Byron stayed, inspired him when writing The Bride of Abydos:

'Know ye the land where the cypress and myrtle.
Are emblems of deeds that are done in their clime?
Where the rage of the vulture, the love of the turtle,
Now melt into sorrow, now madden to crime!'

Byron goes on to describe the character of the people of Turkey, which, after a lengthy stay here strikes you as unchanged to this day!

As you drive South towards Ephesus in spring, you come across fields of pure white cotton frothing like whipped cream from a crown of dark green fringed with coral, which is a wondrous sight.

Further on, large expanses of slender asphodel ripple in the slightest breeze like rose tinted mother of pearl, and fields of opium poppies, white or pale mauve, stretch out of sight as a quivering carpet.

America tried to curb the cultivation of the opium poppy, providing subsidies for an alternative crop, but the agreement did not last long, in spite of American protestations. The picking is still controlled, after a fashion, but the peasant keeps back what is not needed for medicinal purposes and sells it on the side.

A hundred years ago is modern history in a land that counts in millenia. In the mid 1800s the French poet and politician Alphonse de Lamartine, whose popularity was waning after the revolution of 1848, wrote to the Sultan of Turkey suggesting that he might consider gracing that country with his presence, if offered estates and a stipend. The Sultan obliged. Whereupon Lamartine freighted a ship to carry him, his Scottish wife and his possessions to Smyrna, and there hired a camel caravan to travel inland to the property and lands granted by the Sultan, extending from Torbali to Tire, an area of about twenty kilometres, on the road to Ephesus.

His Scottish wife detested the mosquitoes and primitive conditions, which continue more or less unchanged, and within a few days of their arrival they returned the way they had come. In Istanbul a street bears the name of Lamartine.

Further along that road to Ephesus, a rough track leads to a recently excavated tomb; it is believed to be that of Antiochus II, murdered in Ephesus by his wife and half-sister in 246 B.C.

Margaret our Christmas Eve hostess whose husband, a British Army Major was attached to NATO in Izmir, took me to the bazaar of cobbled streets, each hosting a single trade where primitive heating charcoal braziers, mangals, were proudly displayed right outside on to the cobbles, as well as black iron cooking stoves. Most people sent their cakes and roasts to the done at the baker's oven. An entire street specialised in Rahat Lokum (Turkish Delight) stuffed with pistachios or flavoured with rose petal.

In an adjoining street harness makers showed saddles resembling those of cowboys, higher in front and back. Right up to 1948 the best way to travel was on horseback, and horses were trained to amble by hobbling the two feet on one side together, which was deemed a more comfortable pace for long journeys with the rider's legs stretched down, the foot resting on a long wide metal plate. All the harness was lavishly adorned with blue beads against the evil eye, and emitted a strong smell for lack of adequate curing.

While waiting at one of the marble merchant's to collect a black marble coffee table made for Margaret, we sat on chairs hastily dusted of white marble powder, amidst rivulets of milky water trickling from the machine that cut the marble wet to prevent cracking; while muscular men, stripped down to the waist, lifting heavy slabs of marble bandied about to one another endearments such as: *shekerim* (my sugar), *djanem* (my soul), and the ultimate *djiyerim,* (my liver).

In the jeweller's row, pyramids of gold bangles, piled high, like macaroons in a pastry shop, flashed under the electric lighting. They are mainly of 24 carat gold, sold by the weight as dowries to daughters or investment for wives, and are favoured by peasants from the interior on their visits to the big city.

Later, when Margaret had to go to Bayrakli, half way up the bay, to inspect the making of her dining-room chairs by a renowned Italian cabinet-maker, she took me to see, the foundations of old Smyrna, before Alexander the Great rebuilt the town on Mount Pagus, and near by incredibly, we found the tomb of Tantalus!

As we entered the courtyard where the workshop stood, the pastry cook, backing the yard, had just laid a tray of cream cakes on the concrete ground to cool. A stray dog strolled in and had a nibble. The cabinet-maker laughed at our exclamations of horror, as a man rushed out, kicked off the dog, patted the cakes back into shape and placed them in the shop window. When he returned to fill a bowl with milk from a barrel standing in the yard, we were puzzled by the cautious motion of his arm as he spooned it out, and looked inside the barrel where the surface was black with drowned flies. That milk, we shuddered to think, would go in the making of the next batch of cakes.

On a warm sunny day I went with Tantou to Ephesus, which was being re-excavated, since the early 1950s, by the Austrians under Professor Miltner. Tantou, whose insight in any kind of history was extensive, translated, as the local Turkish archaeologist unlocked a small depot where a wonderful jumble of pieces of sculpture, urns and reliefs, lay on the sandy ground. Today's museum was still in the future, but there was an element of expectant discovery in this rough assemblage that no one had yet seen. On the sides of sarcophagi were depicted the battles of the Amazons, rendered in the unique realism of the old masters of ancient Greece, who dressed their models in wet draperies.

It was in 1866 that the English archaeologist H.T. Wood first excavated the Artemision at Ephesus, one of the seven wonders of the ancient world, which was burnt down by a madman in 356 B.C. on the night Alexander the Great was born.

In 1904 H.G. Hogart took up those excavations for the British Museum to which he fortunately sent some of his finds which are now the only ones preserved.

Not only had the Byzantines plundered the site to build the Basilica of Saint John at Ephesus, but later the invading Turks in the 14th century, stripped it of its columns and remaining marbles to build the mosque of Isa Bey, overlooking the now desolate spot where the temple once stood.

In the early 1960s new excavations started at the Basilica of Saint John, thanks to the generosity of an American George B. Quatman, who saw in a dream that his prayers for the recovery of his wife, critically ill, would be answered if he helped to rebuild the Basilica of Saint John at Ephesus.

After founding the American Ephesus Society of Lima Ohio, the press in the United States, gave the enterprise publicity which helped to initiate work on the new dig.

George Quatman had no idea at the outset how much work would be involved. A considerable number of sarcophagi, columns and urns were unearthed, the baptistery, a pool for total immersion, was discovered, but after the site of the altar, over the burial chamber, was rebuilt in white marble as well as one or two arches, funds ran out by the 1970s. It was an immense site, 360 by 130 feet. The Basilica was first built by the Emperor Justinian, in the 6th century, and one man's fortune was quite inadequate for the enterprise.

The Virgin Mary came to Ephesus with Saint John the Disciple (hence the Basilica named after him), and the house where she is believed to have lived at the top of Mount Pion, has been turned into a church where miracles do happen and the crutches of those cured are left beside the altar. Turks believe in Our Lady and Turkey has even issued a postage stamp with the picture of Miryem Anna (Mother Mary).

On the 15th of August, Feast of the Assumption, an open air Mass is said and pilgrims gather from all over the world. Saint Paul preached at Ephesus where a maker of statuettes of Artemis one Demetrius whose trade became threatened as Paul was denouncing the old gods, reported him as an impostor to the Roman authorities, who incarcerated him in a small stone house still standing at the top of a hill.

In 1967 when Pope Paul VI came on an official visit, the remains of the twin churches of the Councils of A.D. 431 and 449, became front page news. Not since the 7th century had a Pope visited these shores, and then only as far as Constantinople. He knelt in prayer on a crimson prie-Dieu, placed in the first of the two churches, where the world's press and television were assembled; then he climbed in a motorcade, to the House of Our Lady 700 metres up the hill.

AMO helped to carry members of the press, and the local archaeologist, who had by then taught himself English, urged a short-cut so that pictures of the Pontiff's arrival could be taken from above. The July heat was terrific, and, in the course of the ascent, the radiator began to splutter. In despair, we had to stop and were gathered helpless round the open bonnet when the Pope's car overtook us. He smiled and waved, seeming amused at our attempt to beat him to the top.

While wandering in the ruins of Ephesus the visitor might come across some historic weeds, such as the acanthus, a long lanky fern which inspired sculptors to carve the Corinthian capitals. Another is the narthex, a tall pinkish resinous plant bearing a cluster of small yellow daisies at the top, which was used in torch light processions and left, when snuffed-out, in the exonarthex of churches, to which it gave its name. Turkish peasants use it to kindle their fires.

On that first visit in 1957 our keen archaeologist showed us the main marble street that had already been excavated; it was adorned with elaborately carved fountains commemorating Roman Emperors, while the opposite side of the street was still embedded under the hill. Further along stood a grandiose bathing establishment known as the Baths of Scolastica, all in white marble and centrally heated. The sumptuous loos of white marble right down to the marble channel at the bottom in which water was continuously running, were arranged in a large square so that men could discuss politics while thus engaged. These establishments also provided entertainments on the floor above, where ladies were ready to oblige.

This, however, was by no means the only centre for such enjoyments as we soon discovered when going up that street; the imprint of a foot carved in one of the marble paving slabs drew our attention, as it was designed to do. The big toe pointed to another place of voluptuous diversions clearly translated in three languages on a board at its entrance, for the enlightment of the tourist:

'Freudenhaus, bordel, brothel'. After that you are well and truly informed. This great expanse of marble has acquired a mellow golden patina not comparable to the cold harshness of the new. Years later, when I came to stay in Izmir, it was fascinating to follow the progress of the excavations revealing more temples, odeons and shops that had been buried under the hill for so many centuries.

Occasionally we were entertained, with a group of friends, by the archaeologist, to peaches and wine, by moonlight that played upon the marbles lending them the sheen of satin. Once we scrambled up a newly uncovered building dating from the second century A.D. with an indoor swimming pool on its higher floor.

AMO was the only car ever to have been driven under a marble arch meant for chariots. We had to hug one side of the street for fear the hollow part, over the Greco-Roman drain underneath, might cave in.

On that first visit in 1957 I acquired exclusive photographs of recent finds, intending to write an article, but events on my return to Ankara prevented me. All my time was taken up by harassing formalities in trying to unfreeze my money. You never got a definite refusal, but vague promises. Days went into weeks and then months while your life ebbed away like sand trickling through your fingers.

CHAPTER 15

Ankara Hosts The Shah of Persia

We had agreed with Tantou that if I obtained my money I would come back and fetch her to drive to England.

We drove back the way we had come, but at Akhisar AMO developed a fault. In the middle of the main street I plunged beneath the bonnet. Experience had taught me a few mechanical tricks. I could clean the plugs, the carburettor and the petrol pump, and also spot loose leads. It was always advisable to do these things in a side lane, away from oncoming traffic, otherwise kindly drivers tried to help, convinced they knew better than a mere woman. Unfortunately they often made things worse. One snag was the low octane petrol which caused engine pinking. Later, when I came to stay longer in the country, I had the cylinder-head lifted, the only cure for this problem.

Now however we were stuck, but luckily along came our old friend *'Qu'a cela ne tienne'* who commandeered a bullock-cart to pull us to the garage. There, not only was the repair done but we were filled up with petrol and payment was refused. The owner, Talat Bey, spoke excellent French, thanks once more to the College Saint Benoit at Istanbul. He claimed to be the grandson of Talat of 'Young Turks' fame, who together with his colleague Enver, had dragged Turkey into the First World War alongside Germany and at the same time had been responsible for the extermination of one million Armenians, in 1915. However his ancestry may be taken with a pinch of salt, for Turks tend to adorn their children with the names of their heroes such as Genghiz, Timur, even Attila, whom they will assure you was a Turk who invaded Europe with his hordes, a Turkish word indeed, from *ordu* (troops).

Hittites and Summerians have also been adopted. Ataturk, who should have known better, lent himself to this deception, so keen was he to give the anonymous masses a background of which they could be proud, and instil the seed of nationalism which was totally lacking. He seems to have surpassed his aim, for present day Turks believe that no one else can be as good as they are.

The new Turkish language devised by university professors approved by Ataturk, has been, to a large extent, deprived of its Arabic etymology in favour of French words Turkified, written phonetically. Once a hairdresser in Izmir remarked in amazement about mizampli *(mise en plis)* 'so the French took it from us, did they?' About one third of the language follows this pattern. Ataturk also circulated a list of suitable surnames from which all Turks had to chose. It was a tremendous achievement for one man to accomplish single handed.

In Ankara, although the Ambassador had left, his South American wife was still there. She would invite me to lunch and put on a record to cheer me up saying dramatically:

"Oh do not get so depressed, they will never unfreeze your money, the last person who tried it, such a nice woman, contracted a heart condition and died here."

I did my best to space the luncheon invitations.

Spring came, and I was still running from one ministry to another, spending sleepless nights trying to work out schemes that never came to anything. Finally my back gave up and I could not move. I recalled that threat that one day I would be paralysed from the waist down. Nur Hanim sent me to see a specialist, who decided to operate even though his London colleague had been against it. "Ah but here we know, we can do these things better" he assured me. I began to wonder hopefully; perhaps they could, and I would get rid of all my troubles. He proposed to start by injections to my spine. Nur Hanim forbade it and urged me to have nothing to do with it, but after reflection, she decided to exploit the new situation to try and unfreeze my money, though I could not at first follow her train of thought.

After a long time and many deliberations she managed something, but it had to be approved by a Commission of Bone Specialists. I appeared before four ancient learned professors. Each one had to examine my back exercising it so thoroughly that you would have sworn they were trying to prove the unbreakability of my spine. When they had done, I was forced to remain prone for a week on my Dunlopillo, lying on the floor, I was then staying in a little garret at the top of the hotel, all I could afford, for Tantou's money was going fast.

In the end when Madame Turhan the assistant of the Belgian Ambassador heard, she arranged for me to be seen by a professor who had studied in Germany. He was incensed by the shilly-shallying of his colleagues and wrote a statement declaring that my complaint could not be treated here but only in Europe where I should go without delay. The very document Nur Hanim had hoped for.

Meanwhile the weather was getting warmer. The arid garden in front of the hotel suddenly broke into green, then flowers appeared where thick snow had lain. And then the police came to find me, having been advised from Istanbul that I had not left the country when I should, months earlier. Nur Hanim telephoned the Chief of Police and I went to see him. He was an intelligent youngish man, and English speaking. When he saw my funny little car outside his office he decided to accompany me to the appropriate police station. Taking his seat in the car, he noticed the newspapers bearing my picture on their front page, with the extraordinary caption: 'She went through Jugoslavia alone and no one touched her!'

He took both papers and read, saying:

"I saw these pictures before, so that is you is it? Well, well." Thanks to his intervention I was given a bona-fide permit to stay for another six months.

I was occasionally taken to the opera but once when 'Figaro qui, Figaro la' was sung in Turkish and became: Figaro burda, Figaro orda, such a mouthful, I had to hide a fit of the giggles behind a handkerchief. I often accompanied Nur Hanim to State banquets and balls where the women were beautifully dressed but looked bored. Perhaps it really was not seemly to smile, though sometimes Nur Hanim would say, hearing young people laugh:

"Good, our people are at last learning to enjoy themselves."

Another puzzle was when she introduced me to someone who was red-haired and florid saying:

"Don't you think he looks Flemish? You would never say he was a Turk!"

To the apparent pleasure of the person concerned. Most probably his mother or grandmother had been in someone's harem against her will, as was the sister of Aristotle Onassis. She was lost in 1922 in the fire of Smyrna and presumed killed; when found by her brother forty years later, she was denied permission to see him.

There was an Anglo-Turkish fortnight coming, arranged by the British Council. Some of the participants from England stayed at the Modern Palas. It was a truly fascinating two weeks, more than welcome in the wilds of Anatolia. Dame Ninette de Valois, founder of the Ankara Ballet soon after the war, gave a talk at the University, and the same evening at a gala performance at the Opera, Dame Margot Fonteyn and Michael Soames danced for our delight, a piece from 'Swan Lake'.

Sir John Betjeman arrived and one memorable evening read his poetry. Sir John Rothenstein of the Tate Gallery talked of art.

Madame Turhan of the Embassy, rang me up to meet her at her house the following morning.

"We are going to see an Under-Secretary of State, friend of my husband's at the Ministry of Finance. He is a most reliable man and speaks excellent French," yet another graduate of the College Saint Benoit.

He was indeed helpful, practical and all the things that Turks are not; telephoning immediately for my file to be sent up to him. You could tell that he was irritated by the general incompetence and I felt hopeful once more. However a few more weeks went by; then I learned, through Madame Turhan, that a Council of Ministers was being convened to decide the exchange rate at which I would receive my money. This being official government business we did not suspect any black-market dabbling, and had no doubt that the official rate would be adhered to, bringing the sum I would receive to seven thousand pounds sterling, but no interest though the funds had been so long frozen. At least the government pocketed that, as they did for the multiple other, much larger sums owed to foreign concerns, who would never see their money, unless they invested within some business in Turkey.

We were now well into July, the heat was terrific. I had been struggling for satisfaction for nearly ten months.

On the international stage Ankara was feverishly preparing to receive the Heads of State of Iran and Iraq. A year earlier in August 1957, Istanbul had hosted King Feizal, the young King of Iraq, his uncle the Prince Regent, and his Prime Minister, together with King Husein of Jordan, to debate the Syrian crises, under the auspices of Loy Henderson of the United States.

Then, in February 1958, the Baghdad Pact was signed. John Foster Dulles of the United States and Selwyn Lloyd of Great Britain officiated on behalf of their governments.

These rulers were to meet in Ankara on the 14th of July 1958. In the evening I thought I would drive up to Kavaklidere, where the reception was taking place in a palace where the President of Turkey,

Celal Bayar, was receiving his guests. The main road was cordoned off but someone suggested to go up Posta Caddesi. The new post office which had only recently opened stood at the bottom. The unmade road which was covered with small blocks of rough stone ready to receive a coat of asphalt, was a terrible surface for tyres but we had seen worse, and never gave it a thought.

At the top I found myself rather isolated on an empty esplanade, like a lily in a vase, with only security men on duty, army and police. They were most helpful and led us to a vantage point where we could have a good look through well-lit windows. Though it never occurred to me at the time, the reception given us was due to our sudden appearance from nowhere. They probably assumed we had a right to be there.

We saw the Shah clearly and his beautiful Empress Soraya. Nur Hanim, always keen on etiquette, urged Soraya to remove her dark glasses:

"....*pour qu'on puisse voir vos jolis yeux*" she told her. She had the most stunning green eyes.

Apparently, when the following day Soraya demanded her accustomed milk bath, her A.D.C. politely but firmly conveyed that the little milk available in the country did not suffice to go round Turkish children.

Having had a good look it seemed prudent not to push our luck too far and we made a move to drive down the hill the way we had come. But our police mentor, never realising the manner of our ascent, conducted us to the road lined with soldiers.

The President's Guard of Honour was at that moment at the airport awaiting the young King of Iraq and his party. Having consulted his opposite number there by telephone and getting the all clear the police officer directed us down the hill. The nearest soldiers, seeing him salute, presented arms, while their comrades followed suit one after another until we reached the bottom. It became rather an uncomfortable drive. When the last of them saluted, we fled to the welcome shadows of the nearest side street.

But the awaited guests never arrived. The news eventually reached Ankara of an army revolt in Baghdad. Soldiers had burst into the Palace grounds and were fired on by loyal troops. The Royal Family and their entourage, who were about to leave for Ankara, rushed out on to the terrace and were shot at point blank range. Nineteen of them were killed while rioters ransacked the British Embassy.

King Feizal of Iraq was barely twenty three. He had succeeded his father at the age of three. While being educated in England at Harrow School, his uncle Prince Abdul Ilah assumed the Regency until the young King was crowned at the age of eighteen in 1953; he was Head of the Arab Federation while his cousin King Husein of Jordan was Deputy Head. The rumour spread that King Husein had stayed behind to put down yet another plot against his person. It was an organised conspiracy aimed at all the leaders of the Baghdad Pact, for soon it was learned there had been an abortive attempt on the Shah's life, but he had safely made it to Ankara.

CHAPTER 16

How Ever Did Goebbels Get Away With It!

At about that time the Ambassador returned briefly for the marriage of his daughter with the heir to a well known English title. Madam Menderes, the Prime Minister's wife arrived for the reception with an A.D.C. carrying her gift of a priceless Turkish rug.

AMO having developed trouble in the steering, we repaired to the Ford garage near the hotel. I sat on a greasy stool waiting for the mechanic's verdict when a regular customer arrived driving a highly polished black limousine. We must have been the only two women drivers in town. A white poodle leaned out of the window wearing chamois leather gloves on its front paws. The driver created quite a stir. Her husband was a high ranking Air Force officer, but she was one of Ataturk's adopted daughters. He had quite a few. One of them studying in Paris at the Sorbonne, in the late 1920s, accompanied by a duenna, had jumped to her death from the train on the return journey. 'Unable' said the French newspapers, 'to face the fate awaiting her' etc. etc. Having decreed that Turks must stick to one wife only, he had to give the example. The newspaper went on: 'as the favourites of French Kings before them, the adopted daughters were given in marriage to those the dictator wished to honour'. So much for the gossip columns.

As for AMO, no sooner had we left the garage than we swerved all over the road. The Chief Engineer at the British Embassy to whom we had an introduction, cried after he had a look at it:

"Och! and ye drove up this 'ere hill with this, me dear? Well, fancy that now!"

The steering column was loose. AMO and I were delighted with this useful contact but the Scotsman dashed our speculations, he was going home:

"I want to get into a shop and find things to buy."

The shortages had got him down, as had living in this uninspiring town.

Most of the government ministers fled to join their families in Istanbul for long weekends, a migration which made my own business drag on further.

I occasionally filled the time of waiting with visits to the National Assembly. Nur Hanim arranged my very first attendance; I sat conspicuously alone in the visitor's balcony facing the Assembly and heard from her later the comments made by Members on my features and anatomy. I then realised that my press card would have enabled me to watch the proceedings from the press gallery at the back.

Though I could hardly understand anything that was said, I gathered the main debate dealt with the call to prayer of the Muezzin. Later Nur Hanim explained. I had indeed seen the Muezzin calling on entering Istanbul, but I was nonetheless surprised by such a subject being debated at the Assembly, knowing the decrees of Ataturk abolishing religious practice. But it was all creeping back a mere thirty years later; most probably it had never been completely eradicated, like the Arabic script, in which bank clerks so often made notes on the side. Now the question was: did the Muezzins who used loud-speakers to make themselves heard above the roar of the traffic, take the trouble to climb the narrow way to the top of the minaret, or did they do it all comfortably from below with a microphone?

In 1957 Muslim Fundamentalism had not taken a hold, and yet the engagement of a young woman was broken off in Ankara, the groom saying: 'How can I marry her when so many men have looked at her face?' But by the mid 1960s, when I stayed in Izmir, more and more shopkeepers were absent at the mosque during business hours. The merchant who was supposed to be fitting my carpets was often away at prayers, so the job took a long time to complete, but one day his assistant asked me to mind the shop so that he too could join his master. On Fridays (the Muslim Sunday) the faithful overflowed outside a particular mosque in the bazaar, to the courtyard and beyond into a flower market. Each man prostrated on his individual prayer mat, wearing a skull-cap or a cloth cap with the peak turned back. European head-gear decreed by Ataturk made it difficult to touch the ground with the forehead, though as he had officially abolished religion the point became irrelevant.

Similarly forced to adopt shoes, the wearers flattened them at the back like babouches, rendering them easier to take off when entering the mosque. Both these habits were discouraged, even to making them an offence. Spitting on the ground was also subject to penalties. You will never see a fat man disporting himself, up and down, in the physical exercises (more strenuous than any done in the army) performed five times a day at mosques. They are all lithe.

I had, during my stay in Ankara, read quite a bit of the Koran in an English translation in Nur Hanim's library, and I was filled with admiration at the way the Prophet had tried to better the lives of his people by using the wrath of Allah, as Ataturk had done wielding the law. He had decreed no alcohol, or the eating of pork, always a health hazard in a hot climate. He had also said: 'Let no tobacco touch your lips' hereby underestimating the guile of his followers, who promptly invented the hubble-bubble in which smoke is filtered through a bottle of water and rises up a long tube to the lips. In Izmir I saw an old tattered hag sporting a long cigarette holder worthy of a film star and was informed that thus 'tobacco did not touch her lips' in accordance with the Prophet's teaching.

However some of the interpretations given to the Prophet's laws are puzzling. Theft is commonplace, and I had to change maids ten times to find one who did not steal. One of them, whose small boy had appropriated a fruit knife, blamed me for leaving it lying about. She claimed justification from the Prophet, whose words she interpreted to mean: 'if you see something near at hand that takes your fancy, you may take it, for if Allah did not mean you to have it he would not have placed if before you'.

To overcome natural self-interest, the Prophet decreed that any man helping to carry another's coffin will advance so many more steps nearer to Paradise. A passer-by spontaneously lending his shoulder to carry a coffin is a common sight.

By the 1970s Muslim Fundamentalism was decidedly gaining ground. Young women covered themselves from head to toe in a trendy revival of the tchartchaf.

When the new Grand Hotel Efes, planned and built by a Turco-German consortium, was opened in Izmir towards the end of the 1960s, Tantou and I were among its first patrons. The staff were trained to perfection by the Germans and Tantou, forced to live here lately by the law freezing the assets of foreigners, liked to escape to its elegant surroundings and pretty gardens. At lunch one day, our favourite waiter advised us in a whisper not to order our usual brand of German beer. It had just come to light, though not yet officially, that the night watchman who had been missing for a week, had been found that morning, drowned, in one of the giant vats. Unfortunately many bottles filled from that vat had already been sold.

A year later there was a cholera scare. In a country where anything can be had by bribery, inoculations to obtain a certificate were compulsory at a state Public Centre only. Tantou's Spanish-Jewish doctor provided us with a syringe and the drug and told us how long to boil the needle to sterilise it. We took along our little Greco-Turkish dressmaker and her elderly father. The centre indicated was in the corridors of a cinema in the populous bazaar, where trestles were covered with newspaper upon which stood open, unmarked bottles, cotton wool and little methylated spirit lamps. A dense crowd of peasants pressed on all sides, - the men wearing the baggy trousers which inspired the fashion in the West in 1988, - queuing for hasty jabs by medical students wearing clothes as grubby as the crowd. We carefully chose the cleanest looking student, the dressmaker having threatened one other with her umbrella and a few choice words in Turkish. He selected a bottle at random hoping for surgical spirit, the dressmaker's umbrella stopped him. I lit a match which failed to ignite the cotton; it was the wrong bottle.

"Zarar Yok" he was willing to try again.

When it came to boiling the needle we watched, hawk-eyed, timing the procedure. There was no epidemic of cholera after all, but many people died from infection caused by the injections, as was shown at the time on British Television.

By the spring of 1958 in Ankara, debates in the National Assembly seemed to be getting angrier, and from the press gallery I once saw them come to blows. On another occasion the Opposition accused the Prime Minister Adnan Menderes so viciously that he sprang to his feet, cried:

"Yalan, yalan!" (lies) and walked out of the chamber.

Ishmet Inönü, the leader of the Opposition had quite a following, especially in the armed forces, whom the present regime had neglected to cultivate. Another of their mistakes was the relaxing of the laws against religion, which gained them votes. The armed forces viewed this with misgivings and rallied more and more round the Pasha (general) Inönü who had been Ataturk's number one.

When I had an interview with Kasim Gülek, General Secretary of the Opposition Party, I heard about these problems. He owned most of the National newspapers and was a great landowner in the South, speaking eight languages, including Russian; he had studied at the Sorbonne, at Cambridge, in the United States and Berlin. When I asked what were his hobbies, he replied:

"Women," and took me to dinner at Ataturk's model farm open air restaurant.

As we got up to leave, he gave me his arm, and as we walked between a double row of bowing waiters, he said:

"You can write that you dined with the next Prime Minister."

Towards the middle of August, Madame Turhan told me that she had heard from the Under Secretary of State. They were going to release my money. The document was actually at the Prime Minister's office for signature. It could remain there for months at the bottom of a pile, unless someone helped to place it near the top. No decision could be taken without the prime Minister's consent. Eventually I got an introduction to his private secretary, who spoke English and promised on the telephone to move my paper to the top of the pile. Another feverish wait and speculation. Finally we heard before the month was over that it had been signed and returned to the Ministry of Finance who however, knew nothing about it.

I had by now reached breaking point. It was then that I was sent to the Prime Minister's Eminence Grise, a kind man, tall and distinguished who reigned in an excessively large office decorated like a theatre decor for the Phantom of the Opera, in black and silver. No, he did not have my paper. It was at the Ministry of Finance. As I sat there exhausted, tears began to roll unchecked down my cheeks. The poor man tried to console me in broken English:

"Do not be sorry Madam, do not be sorry" he kept saying.

His secretary came in, made a few telephone calls. The paper was definitely at the Ministry of Finance. Please to go back there again. I arrived too late; it had just closed.

When confirmation of the paper's signature had reached us, I tentatively booked for AMO and myself a passage on a ship from Istanbul to Brindisi. The situation being so very vague, I could not make definite arrangements for Tantou to join us.

The following morning I was back at the Ministry of Finance. The department in question was in the anti-chamber of the Minister. The message from the Eminence Grise had reached and alerted them. Eventually a little man was fetched who unlocked a drawer at his writing table and reluctantly produced a long envelope upon which was stamped in red: 'Prime Minister's Office. Top Secret'; and so he had hidden it and removed the key. It could have been there still. It goes without saying that it took time, twenty four hours, to persuade him to part with it. I had to go back the next day. When he finally released the document on the Saturday morning, I took it to the Head of the Exchange Control downstairs. An iceberg of a man whom not even Nur Hanim had managed to thaw.

He read the paper, mused and laid it open at the top of a pile. He would have to see, better come back later... at that moment his attention was urgently required in the room next door.

I slipped out, ran to the floor above, brushed the attendant out of my way and burst into the office of the Under Secretary of State, friend of Madame Turhan. As I entered the room I blurted out in French:

"In this Ministry, your right hand doesn't know what your left hand is doing. Now that dreadful man down at the Exchange Control is trying to put me off, oh!..."

Before I finished speaking he had the dreadful man on the line.

"Go down now and get your paper. He must sign it, and give it to you. Take it at once to the Central Bank and they will give you the money. Go now, quickly."

When I re-entered his office, the dreadful man's face was puce with rage. He informed me that out of the seven thousand pounds sterling, I would get only two thousand, according to the rate of exchange that had been decided, unless, he added spitefully, I preferred to wait for a more favourable rate and draw the money monthly.

I asked to telephone my Ambassador. At the end of the line I could hear him thinking; then slowly, carefully he said:

"Un tient vaut mieux que deux tu l'auras" - the French equivalent of 'A bird in the hand...'

No one listening in could possibly understand. I got the idea.

When the paper was at long last handed to me, I realised that the essential permit to use the money to buy my travel ticket, was not with it. Bowing low, my persecutor opened the door to let me out, and with a sarcastic grin:

"See what you can do without."

You could only buy a ticket to travel out of the country with foreign currency. Turkish money was not accepted. In this instance permission had to be given by the Exchange-Control.

AMO took me down the boulevard to the Central Bank. There were many directors there, and over them all presided the General Director, almost as powerful as the Prime Minister himself.

I went straight to the director I knew well, who had tried hard to get my expenses paid. He had trained two years at a City bank in London.

When I handed him the paper, he laid it on his desk and looked at me speechless.

"I never thought I would live to see such a paper on my desk," he finally breathed, "So you have done it at last! Good heavens!"

It had never been done before, he told me, and would probably never be repeated.

"Yes but look at the sum, it is stealing, how could they stoop to do such a thing!"

He seemed mesmerised by my document and only came down to earth on hearing I did not get the permit to buy my ticket. He looked up at the clock. It was past twelve noon on a Saturday. Everything closed at one o'clock, including Cooks travel office, where I had booked my ticket.

"Who did your booking, a man or a woman?"

"Woman,"

"I wonder," he said calling his clerk to fetch the money.

"Now we shall see. During the war, I used to listen to the propaganda broadcasts from Germany, I was constantly amazed how Goebbels got away with that pack of lies and deception. But he did time and again. He dared and that's probably half the battle, to dare the impossible; I often wondered whether anyone else could do it?" he remained thoughtful.

The money was brought, he counted it, and I signed the receipt. Then he picked up the telephone.

"We shall now try a Goebbels," he dialled a number.

"Yes, this is the Director of the Central Bank. Are you the young lady who reserved a passage for Miss Creon and her car? Right, well Miss Creon has obtained permission from the Prime Minister to get her money, we are now paying it to her. However, as there is so little time before you close, will you kindly dictate to me exactly what you need from us to issue her with a ticket. We shall then draft a permit at once and send her to you."

He wrote as she spoke, then read it back to her.

"Right, this will be signed and stamped at once, and she will be on her way. Be so kind as to prepare the ticket meanwhile." He rang off triumphant.

"As you know this permit must be given by the Exchange Control. However so far it seems to have worked. Run, get that ticket, jump into your car, go to the nearest port and get on the ship. By Monday or Tuesday when they find out, it will be too late, you'll be far away at sea. Good luck. Drop me a line from London."

When I reached Cooks next to the hotel it was seven minutes to one. The ticket was ready. I handed my permit from the Director. The girl looked at it, then at me, hesitated. My heart sank.

"Have you a Press Card?" she asked.

I produced my press card apprehensively.

"I thought so" she smiled, "you'll get fifty per cent reduction with it."

A clerk was waiting to lock the door after me. I dashed to the hotel, stuffed my things into a case and off we went, from the heights of Ankara (850 metres) hurtling down meandering narrow roads towards Istanbul. The road was dry and dusty now and much easier to negotiate. We reached the Consulate in Istanbul after midnight and Matteo came to open the gate. Inside, he decided it was too late to get permission from the Consul for me to stay at the Consulate, but he was sure that was the safest way and would be approved. I was telling him my story as he made me a bed. The next day Sunday he came to see me safely on the ship. I think he feared someone might even then try to stop me.

From Brindisi I sent a cable to Tantou: 'All's well forced change plans please cable date your arrival London.'

I also posted the letter I had written on the boat to Nur Hanim, suggesting she raised a question at the Assembly that a street should be named after me, being a benefactor of the State, to the tune of five thousand pounds sterling. A very substantial sum in 1958, it could buy you almost three houses. I wondered whether she had the time to do so in view of the imminent fall of the Government in dramatic circumstances.

So in the end it turned out a grab-and-run job, as that young reporter from The Express had suggested before I left London.

Battered but still running at the end of nearly a year's exhausting, gruelling and often hazardous adventures AMO and I crawled back to Britain. It had been a 'successful' foray to retrieve a crumb of the family fortunes.

However, by 1960 we were on our way back to Izmir to stay, for as Tantou said ruefully when she joined us in London, 'five thousand pounds a time is rather a high price to pay to recover only two!'

Addendum

LONDON ISTANBUL WITHOUT EVEN A SCREWDRIVER

On a return visit to Izmir in May 1960 I came across Prime Minister Adnan Menderes when he was laying the foundation stone to a future university at Bornova near Izmir.

I was able to take a close up of him, too close, for he suddenly turned round and spoke to me in French smilingly.

This proved to be a tragic meeting and the last picture of him as a free man, for a few hours later he was arrested in the course of a military coup, and incarcerated. Later, after a ghastly trial that must forever remain a blot on the history of modern Turkey, he was hanged, and so was his Minister of Finance, that same Hasan Polatkan with whom I had an interview in Ankara in 1957 in connection with the unfreezing of my funds.

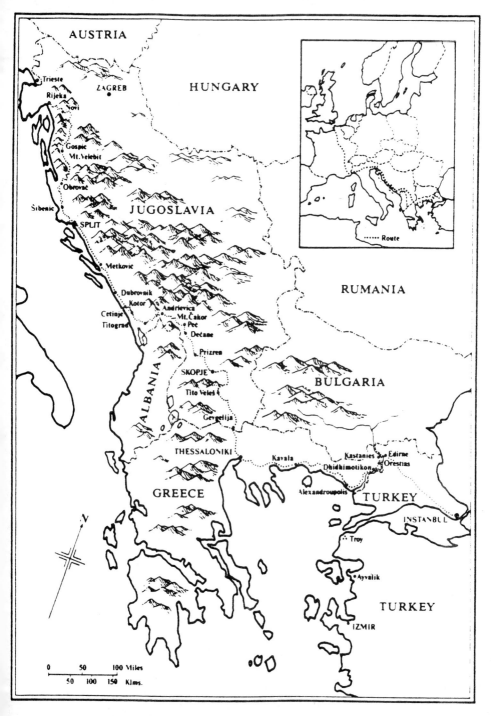

A Map of Jugoslavia showing the route
followed from Riejka to Istanbul.

A Map of Jugoslavia showing the route
followed from Riejka to Istanbul.